Charles Gross, Ernest Lavisse

General View of the Political History of Europe

Charles Gross, Ernest Lavisse

General View of the Political History of Europe

ISBN/EAN: 9783337071714

Printed in Europe, USA, Canada, Australia, Japan

Cover: Foto ©Suzi / pixelio.de

More available books at **www.hansebooks.com**

GENERAL VIEW

OF THE

POLITICAL HISTORY OF EUROPE

BY

ERNEST LAVISSE
PROFESSOR AT THE SORBONNE

TRANSLATED WITH THE AUTHOR'S SANCTION BY

CHARLES GROSS, PH.D.
INSTRUCTOR IN HISTORY, HARVARD UNIVERSITY

NEW YORK

LONGMANS, GREEN, AND CO.
15 EAST SIXTEENTH STREET

1891

TRANSLATOR'S PREFACE.

THE title of Professor Lavisse's work is *Vue Générale de l'Histoire Politique de l'Europe.* (Third edition. Paris : Armand Colin & Co. 1890.) While giving the essential facts of universal history, he aims, above all, to describe the formation and political development of the states of Europe, and to indicate the historical causes of their present condition and mutual relations. In other words, he shows how the existing political divisions of Europe, with their peculiar tendencies, were created. To accomplish this, it was necessary to begin with the history of Greece and Rome, which played an important part in Europe long after their death ; then, to show the potent influence of the Holy Roman Empire and of the Papacy in the Middle Ages ; next, to point out how these two great ideal powers were superseded by modern Europe, an organic entity composed of various states, new and old, most of which were dominated by the monarchical idea ; and, finally, how, in the nineteenth century, the new principle of nationality and the power of the people have supplanted the old monarchical element. The ability of Professor Lavisse to compress the essence of a great event or sequence of events into a few comprehensive and expressive sentences, has enabled him to accomplish his difficult task with signal success. At any rate, this is the opinion of the Translator, and hence he believes that the work will prove useful to general readers, as well as to college students, in America and England.

The Translator has attempted to adhere as closely to the original as the English idiom permits. He has, however, taken the liberty to divide the work into chapters and sections, and to make some slight changes in the titles of the sections; he has also added an Index.

He desires to express his thanks to the friends who have kindly aided him with suggestions, especially to Professor A. B. Hart, of Harvard College, and Professor A. G. Canfield, of Kansas State University.

CAMBRIDGE, MASS.
October 1, 1891.

AUTHOR'S PREFACE.

WHEN a writer presents to the public a *General View of the Political History of Europe,** he exposes himself to the reproach of having undertaken too much. We know, at the present day, the trouble and care that are necessary to establish the truth of a single fact. How, then, can anyone aspire to deal with the great mass of facts that make up the political history of Europe?

The historians who, nevertheless, venture to treat such subjects, can say in their defence that if the details are often doubtful, the leading facts are not. We do not know with complete certainty the inner motives of Luther's revolt, and there are obscurities in the history of the battle of Waterloo; but it is certain that Luther revolted, and that the battle of Waterloo was lost by Napoleon. Now

---

* The idea of this volume was suggested to me by a preface which I wrote in 1886 for the translation of one of Mr. Freeman's books (Historical Geography of Europe, by Edward A. Freeman, translated by Mr. Gustave Lefèvre, under the title, *Histoire Générale de l'Europe par la Géographie Politique.* Paris: Armand Colin & Co.). It seemed to me that it might be useful to expand this first undertaking into a book.

these two events had results that are very clear
and very important.

Decisive events, those that can be said to belong
to universal history, are rare. It is not impossible
to discern them, to understand them, and to per-
ceive their results. It is for this reason, paradox-
ical as the opinion may seem, that the *generic* in
history is more certain than the *specific*. It is
easier to be deceived concerning a person than concerning a whole country. The view that fails to
distinguish individual trees takes in the whole for-
est; the vastest horizons are the clearest. Nevertheless, an attempt, like the present, to sketch in a
few pages the history of so many centuries, is not
wholly devoid of peril. Certain opinions and
judgments that are briefly expressed may aston-
ish, perhaps even offend, the reader.

Let me also beg him to choose carefully his
point of view in this stretch of three thousand
years. We are tempted to exaggerate certain
facts, because, for our own special reasons, they
arouse our interest more than others. We are better acquainted with ancient history and with the
centuries of the Renaissance, of Louis XIV., and
of Voltaire, than with the Middle Ages and the
nineteenth century. This is one of the effects of
our education. Nevertheless, in the Middle Ages
were formed the rudiments of the nations, whose
development has been completed in the course of

the present century. These two periods are thus the most important in the history of Europe—I mean political history, properly speaking.

This volume presents the sequence of the great phenomena of history, and it also attempts to give the *how* of things. It would be well to add the *why*, if it were not too bold an undertaking.

Nature has written on the map of Europe the destiny of certain regions. She determines the aptitudes and, hence, the destiny of a people. The very movement of events in history creates, moreover, inevitable exigencies, one thing happening because other things have happened. On the other hand, nature has left, on the map of Europe, free scope to the uncertainty of various possibilities. History is full of accidents, the necessity of which cannot be demonstrated. Finally, there exists free power of action, which has been exercised by individuals and nations.

Chance and freedom of action oppose alike the fatality of nature and the fatality of historical sequence. To what extent each of these four elements has influenced history cannot be determined with exactness. Still it may be interesting, at least, to attempt to accomplish something in this direction. My little volume invites the reader to make such an attempt.

One word more. I have done my best to guard myself against the prejudices of patriotism, and I believe that I have not exaggerated the place of France in the world's history. But the reader will find that, in the conflict between the opposing factors of history, France is the most formidable adversary of the fatality of historical sequence. A century ago she placed herself athwart the course of European events, and precipitated it into a new direction. At the present day we feel a formidable fatality weighing upon the Continent of Europe; hence this book closes with some pessimistic pre-dictions. But it points out in its last pages, that if the discord which is arming Europe, and threatens to ruin her, can be appeased, it will be done by the spirit of France.

ERNEST LAVISSE.

January, 1890.

CONTENTS.

CHAPTER I.

ANCIENT HISTORY.

CHAPTER II.

TRANSITION TO MEDIÆVAL HISTORY.

CHAPTER III.

THE MIDDLE AGES.

CHAPTER IV.

· MODERN TIMES.

CHAPTER V.

THE NINETEENTH CENTURY.

POLITICAL HISTORY OF EUROPE.

CHAPTER I.

ANCIENT HISTORY.

§ 1. *General Characteristics.*

A PEOPLE does not possess a history by the mere fact of its existence; its life must be active and fruitful.

An historical people is one which has rules for the guidance of its political and social life, and which has some measure of order in its government and of justice in its society. It professes religion and morality. It is skilled in the work of the hands and of the mind : it has industries, art, and literature. It comes in contact with other nations in order to use its powers, to enrich itself, and to gratify its pride, devoting itself to commerce or to conquest, or to both at once.

At the present day several nations deserve to be called historical; the actions of each of them and their mutual relations constitute history. But the farther back we go, the rarer are such nations. At first there was in Europe only one, the Greeks; after them only one occupied the scene—a scene of wider dimensions—the Romans.

The history of Greece and Rome forms our first period, which closes about the fourth century of the Christian era; then new actors appear, the Germans and Slavs, to give complexity to history, which till then was very simple.

§ 2. *Greece.*

It was natural that the history of Europe should begin in the southeast, quite close to the cradle of the earliest civilizations.

Greece turned to account the experience acquired by the nations which inhabited the valleys of the Euphrates and the Tigris, the slopes of Mount Lebanon, and the banks of the Nile. But Grecian civilization was distinguished from that of earlier nations by an excellence that may be called European, namely, by independent activity.

It was also natural that Greece should at once acquire the characteristic features of European civilization. This country, which receives the ocean in the sinuosities of its shores and thrusts its promontories into the ocean, this peninsula, encompassed by islands and cut up by valleys with dominating plains, is like a reduced copy of our peninsular-shaped continent, with its extensive coast and well-defined bays. Greece, in short, is Europe reflected and condensed in a mirror.

Her history likewise foretells that of Europe. Greece was divided into populations related to, and yet differing from, one another. Her cities were small sovereign states, which in their mutual intercourse employed all the combinations of politics. Two or three of them exercised a hegemony, which, however, was never extensive or durable.

She succeeded in organizing within the sacred precincts of her cities a government and a society. She excelled in all kinds of human activity—poetry, philosophy, science, art, industry, and commerce. The powers thus acquired she diffused abroad. Along the whole Mediterranean coast, from the Euxine to the Columns of Hercules, she founded cities, which were offspring of her own towns; but just as she was never consolidated into a state, so, too, she did not unite her colonies into an empire. When, however, she lost her power of action, and fell under the rule of a military people, the Macedonians, Grecian states were formed; but the most important of them were in Asia and Egypt.

Greece, however, was destined to survive in Europe, where Hellenism, under different forms, long continued to exercise very great influence.

It modified the customs and ideas of republican Rome. After the foundation of Constantinople it created a religious and political civilization, the Byzantine. It broke up Roman unity in the last days of the Empire. During the Middle Ages it was antagonistic to the ideas and systems of which the West made trial, and it destroyed the ecclesiastical unity of the Christian world. Still later, in the period of the Renaissance, its wide diffusion rejuvenated thought, and produced the intellectual development of modern times.

§ 3. *The Roman Dominion.*

The Italian Peninsula does not resemble that of Greece. It is more regular in outline; islands do not abound around the coast; and its inlets do not face the East. Italy is, moreover, situated in the centre of the Mediterranean, and Sicily brings her within view of Africa. She is much more continental, in the language of French sailors more *terrienne*, than Greece. Her indigenous inhabitants along the coast came in contact with foreign seamen. It was, however, a city of husbandmen that united them all under its laws.

Rome employed the first centuries of her existence in enlarging her territory, just as a peasant rounds off his estate. Like all conquerors, she continued to conquer because she had begun to conquer. Her first wars led to others; her first successes rendered the later ones at once necessary and easy. She finally believed that it was her mission to conquer other nations. Conquest became to her a profession :

Tu regere imperio populos, Romane, memento.

She thus considerably extended the field of history, by bringing within its limits Spain, Gaul, Britain, the country situated between the Alps and the Danube, and a part of Germany. To exploit these conquered territories she invented the *province.*

Her administration destroyed the ancient nations, and fused the old historical and natural divisions into the unity of the *orbis romanus.* This name she gave to the beautiful Mediterranean region in the centre of which arose " the immovable rock of the Capitol." The Grecian cities had separately founded colonies ; Greece dispersed her strength : Rome consolidated the world—in the words of Varro, *fiebat orbis urbs.* There had been a Grecian world, but not a Grecian empire ; there was a Roman world, and also a Roman empire.

Rome's activity was intense and profound. She transformed nations, substituted order for anarchy, and taught the conquered people her language, customs, and religion. She rose to the conception of *genus humanum,* and wrote human reason in her laws. One cannot help admiring so extraordinary a power, but it is doubtful whether all its influences were beneficent.

All uniformity of education is dangerous, because individual divergence is necessary for the progress of human activity. The more competing individuals there are, the more productive is the world's work. As far as she could, Rome destroyed the individual genius of nations; she seems to have rendered them unqualified for a national existence. When the public life of the Empire ceased, Italy, Gaul, and Spain were thus unable to become nations. Their great historical existence did not commence until after the arrival of the barbarians, and after several centuries of experiments amid violence and calamity.

The countries that Rome civilized do not owe her thanks only. We are fond of contrasting the picture of Celtic Gaul with that of Roman Gaul. The villages are transformed into cities, huts into palaces, foot-paths into paved ways, uncultured orators into eloquent rhetoricians, and barbarous warriors into generals and emperors. We marvel at this miracle, and at the happy life that people led in the Gallo-Roman cities.

But how does it happen that the countries which Rome did not conquer, or did not long have under her sway, now hold such a prominent place in the world—that they exhibit so much originality and such complete confidence in their future? Is it only because, having existed a shorter time, they are entitled to a longer future? Or, perchance, did Rome leave behind her certain habits of mind, intellectual and moral qualities, which impede and limit activity? These are insolvable questions, like all similar ones whose solution it would be important for us to know. At any rate, let us not be too prompt to pass judgment in this matter. It is not certain that Cæsar's conquest of Vercingetorix was a blessing to the world.

§ 4. *Division into Two Empires.*

Though strongly organized, this vast dominion encountered various opposing forces which it could not overcome.

Very frequently there was opposition, and hence permanent conflict, between the spirit of the North and that of the South. But in Roman times the North was only an external enemy, and one which was held in check. The real contrast lay between the West and the East—the West, which Rome had subdued and assimilated by civilizing it; the East, which still retained its Hellenic civilization.

Into Western Europe Rome introduced her spirit and language; but from Hellenism she won with great difficulty Southern Italy and Sicily. The language and civilization of Greece survived from the Adriatic to Mount Taurus. In this stretch of country the Roman name displaced the Grecian, but it was Roman only in appearance. On the day when Constantine founded a second Rome, an empire began which the Byzantine chancery called the Roman Empire, but which history regards as the Greek Empire.

The separation of the West and the East was inevitable, and was consummated when, in the year 395, the two sons of Theodosius began to reign, the one at Ravenna, the other at Constantinople. From that time there existed two distinct states, each with it own task and its own enemies—the latter forming a great and potent throng that strove to make room for itself on the scene of action.

§ 5. *Causes of the Fall of Rome.*

It was not the division into two empires, nor merely the power of external enemies, that destroyed the domination of Rome. Republican Rome had ended in monarchy by the decadence of her institutions and customs, by the very effect of her victories and conquests, by the necessity of giving to this immense dominion a *dominus*. But after she had begun to submit to the reality of a monarchy, she retained the worship of republican forms.

The Empire was for a long time a piece of hypocrisy; for it did not dare to give to its rulers the first condition of stability, a law of succession. The death of every emperor was followed by troubles, and the choice of a master of the world was often left to chance. At length the monarchy had to be organized, but thenceforth it was absolute, without restraint or opposition. Its proposed aim was to exploit the world, an aim which in practice was carried to an extreme. Hence it exhausted the *orbis romanus.*

We may also mention among the causes of ruin the very duration of the Empire, the wear and tear of time. The world felt itself growing old. It was seeking and awaiting something new. This it could not obtain by a political revolution, for no one thought of any other form of government than the empire; nor by a social revolution, for the mind had become inured to the régime of castes that had gradually secured a foothold. A religious revolution occurred, but it was directed against the Empire. To say, "My kingdom is not of this world," was to hurl divine contempt at the pagan world, which desired to be self-sufficing, and did not recognize the existence of a future life. To say, "Render to Cæsar the things that are Cæsar's, and to God the things that are God's," was to distinguish God from Cæsar, in whom were blended the human and the divine.

This distinction having once been made, would not the debt to God have been much greater than the obligation to Cæsar? To say, " Heaven and earth shall pass away," was to gainsay the prediction of the Empire's eternity (*Imperium sine fine dedi*); to speak thus was to shake the immovable rock.

CHAPTER II.

§ 1. *General Characteristics.*

FROM the East, the cradle of races, the tumultuous procession of the nations advances—Germans, Slavs, Huns, Avars, and Arabs. They differ very much from one another. Humanity with its contrasting variations, congenital or slowly acquired, enters into conflict with the Roman work of assimilating men by force and by the power of the intellect.

The Arabs were characterized by a potent originality. They represented the great Semitic race as opposed to the great Aryan race. They founded a religion and an empire, and did not harmonize with the imperial Roman past. They have, in fact, a peculiar domicile of their own in history.

The Huns and the Avars, both of the Turanian race, more poorly endowed than the Semites, untouched by earlier educating influences, still remaining in the primitive state of nomads, and

benighted in fetichism, brought with them nothing
save brutality.   Destroyers, incapable of founding
anything, they were destined to be destroyed.

The Germans and the Slavs are of the same
stock as the Greeks and Romans.   Posted on the
frontiers of the Roman Empire, where dwelt
order, joy, and wealth, it seemed as though they
were simply awaiting the time when they were to
divide their patrimony.   They are the younger
branches of the Aryan family, which succeeded
when the older ones were exhausted and withered.

All these nations, differing in origin, customs,
and religion, came in contact with the Roman
Empire.   In the East, it suffered encroachment
without being destroyed; in the West, the Germans, after unintentionally extinguishing the Empire, restored it.   In the year 800, when Charlemagne was crowned in the basilica of St. Peter,
Europe appeared to be again restored to good
order, as in the time of Theodosius, with her
two capitals, Rome and Constantinople.   This
was the case only in appearance; but appearances
are facts, and illusions are powers that produce
real actions of considerable importance.

Thus the year 800 marks the end of a second
period.   Let us now trace the history of Europe
to this date.

§ 2. *The Empire of the East.*

The main efforts of the barbarians were directed against the West. A few years after the death of Theodosius, Britain was abandoned by the Roman legions. Franks, Visigoths, and Burgundians occupied Gaul and Spain. Almost all the barbarians visited and pillaged Italy. Groups of mercenaries established their quarters in the Peninsula, but no people took possession of it in the formal way in which the above-mentioned tribes occupied Gaul. Italy inspired respect. Though completely disarmed, she was protected by the grand reminiscences of her glory, just as Sylla had formerly been shielded by the shades of his proscribed victims. No king entertained the idea of reigning over Rome. Emperors continued to succeed one another, valiant or craven, intelligent or stupid, all equally impotent.

Nevertheless, in the year 476, the chief of the mercenaries of Italy, Odoacer by name, thought that it was no longer necessary that the West should have a separate emperor. He caused the imperial insignia to be carried to Gaul by a deputation charged to tell the Emperor Zeno that a single master of the world sufficed.

Thenceforth unity, as it existed under the Cæsars and Antonines, seemed to be restored. Con-

stantinople imagined that in the future she alone
was to direct the course of history. There the
Emperor received the homage of the kings of the
West. He sent titles and favors to the limits of
the *orbis romanus.* He decorated Clovis, King of
the Franks, with the insignia of a proconsul.

Against Odoacer, the Emperor sent to Italy the
Ostrogoths, commanded by Theodoric, who, will-
ingly or unwillingly, remained his lieutenant. At
one time it even seemed as though the Emperor
were going to take effective possession of the
world; for Justinian conquered Italy, Africa, a
part of Spain, and various islands and shores of
the Western Mediterranean.

This return to offensive operations on the part
of the ancient power was of short duration. The
Lombards, invading Italy in the sixth century,
wrested from the Empire all save a few islets of
territory, and these were beaten and wasted by
the waves of the invasion. The Arabs, by their
conquests in Asia, Africa, and Spain, formed an
immense semicircle around the *orbis romanus* on
the south.

Relegated to the East, the Empire, still calling
itself the universal Empire, began to assume the
well-defined character of an oriental state. Barbarian invasions complicated the ethnography of
the Balkan Peninsula. The Slavs spread over
the north and the northwest; and thus Servia

and Croatia came into existence. Istria and Dal-
matia were completely permeated with Slavs, who
likewise penetrated by infiltration into Macedonia
and Greece. The Bulgarians, a Turanian people,
who were soon assimilated by the Slavs, crossed
the Danube, and spread out far beyond the Balkans. Such is the agglomeration of elements out
of which was to arise the modern Eastern Question.

Henceforth there was no longer any hope of restoring the universal empire. Only a modest
function remained to be performed by the Byzantine Empire : it had to strive to exist. It is a
marvel that it existed so long.

§ 3. *The Western Barbarians and the Church.*

While the East thus adhered to the forms of the
past, new and curious experiments were being
tried in the West. These novelties were not of a
revolutionary nature. When the Germans first
entered into relations with Rome, they came in
the attitude of armed supplicants, demanding
lands in exchange for their military service. Ma-
rius destroyed this first army of invaders, but
others came, always repeating the same supplica-
tions. The frontiers of the Rhine and the Danube,
after a long defence, gave way. Numerous individuals, bands more or less considerable, finally

whole nations, came for the purpose of establishing themselves on Roman soil.

In the course of the fifth century the Visigoths, Burgundians, and Franks divided Gaul; and the Ostrogoths occupied Italy. None of them were destroyers. Each of these nations, spread out over vast provinces, formed a minority in the midst of a completely Roman population, and sought to live in harmony with the latter. In this attempt they showed some intelligence and much good-will, but they could not cast off their old customs.

The government of the barbarian kings was a peculiar monarchy, half Roman, half German, absolute in principle, but tempered by revolts, by murders, and, above all, by the impossibility of their comprehending the spirit of imperial government. The surviving respect for the Empire disturbed the Ostrogoths, established on soil pre-eminently Roman, and also the Burgundians, whose chancery makes them use the language of very humble servants when they address the Emperor of the East. Nevertheless, this sentiment, which the people of the West professed for the Empire, was a superstition. It was a new power that was destined to give the barbarians a domicile in history.

The Christian Church, after having lived concealed in the Empire, after having defied its laws and suffered its persecutions, had received from it honors, privileges, riches, and a model for her government. In fact, the imperial hierarchy was re-produced in the cities by the bishops, and in the provinces by the metropolitans. The Bishop of Rome, successor of St. Peter and sole patriarch of the West, already saluted with the title of universal bishop, was spiritually what the successor of Augustus was temporally.

Thus the Church remade, or rather perpetuated, the idea of universality. When the Roman father-land, torn into fragments, was about to be super-seded by many small countries, the Church offered to civilized humanity the great ecclesiastical and Christian fatherland. She mediated a quiet tran-sition from the past to the future. Was she not in reality Roman? Her leader sat at Rome; her language was that of Rome; and her worship had become the official worship of Rome. The words "Christian" and "Roman" were at first opposed to each other. When the martyrs refused to wor-ship at the statue of the Emperor, they justified their disobedience by saying: "I am a Christian," *Sum Christianus.* But in the fourth century the two words approached each other in meaning or were confused; "Christian" and "Roman" be-came, in fact, synonymous terms.

Like ancient Rome, the Church conquered and assimilated. The intellectual sap of the ancient world no longer produced anything but miserable flowerets without color or perfume. The Church,

2

on the other hand, attracted intelligent men by her literature, history, dialectics, the philosophy of her dogma, and her words of eternal life.

Since the barbarians did not wish to destroy Rome, since they entered the Empire as guests, and since they were not numerous enough or strong enough to exterminate the ancient population or to reduce it to obedience, they had no other policy to adopt save to make it accept them. But the necessary and prime condition of this step was their own acceptance by the Church. Accordingly, the Visigoths, Burgundians, Vandals, and Ostrogoths consented to become Christians, but after their own fashion. They did not accept the whole Catholic creed. Hence they were merely transient figures on the scene of action. The Church and the Roman population were not powerful enough to drive them away, but they allowed Justinian to obtain possession of Italy, and aided the Franks to conquer Gaul and the West.

§ 4. *The Franks.*

The Franks had long been familiar with the name of Rome, and had, in fact, been in her service, but they had not been Romanized like the Visigoths and Burgundians. They were no longer wholly barbarians, although still uncivilized. Established on the northern frontier of the Empire, they occupied territory partly Roman and partly German. Inhabiting both sides of the Rhine, which separated the classical from the barbarian world, they were destined to be the medium of communication between the past, in which the chief actors were the Romans, and the future, which was to be mainly the possession of the Germanic nations.

Like the Church, the Franks were thus capable of mediating a transition. Hence the harmony between the ecclesiastical power and Frank energy is one of the greatest facts in universal history. The vigor of the Franks by itself would have sufficed to triumph over the worn-out and enervated Visigoths and Burgundians; but the baptism of Clovis and his policy toward the Church completed the success of the Franks. St. Remi gave them citizenship among the Roman populations, in whose midst the other barbarians remained strangers because they were heretics.

The Church immediately opened to their ambition an immense perspective. She sought a new people of God, which she could charge with the divine mission. Hence on the day after the baptism of Clovis priests preached to the new David concerning his duties; the task which they imposed upon him was nothing less than to unite under one law and one faith all the nations of the earth.

Beyond the ancient limits of the Empire the Franks conquered Alemannia and Thuringia; they also made Bavaria a dependent state; and Christianity began to be preached in these new countries. But the Franks did not immediately succeed in accomplishing their arduous task. The Merovingian dynasty governed poorly, and never even succeeded in comprehending what a government was. It wore itself out in enjoyments, discords, and imbecile follies. Its empire was dismembered · Neustria, Aquitaine, Burgundy, Austrasia, Alemannia, and Bavaria secured separate organizations. In each of these provinces, which were like distinct kingdoms, little groups of seigneurs with their dependents began to be absorbed in their own local life.

Among these seigneurs were the bishops. Having become great landowners and important members of the state, they were entangled and lost in the temporal hierarchy. It seemed as though the world would split into an infinite number of small pieces. But the idea of unity survived in the great pagan reminiscences, in the indestructible power of the imagination, and in the creed of the Bishop of Rome, the successor of that apostle to whom Christ had entrusted the task of feeding the universal flock of the faithful.

At the close of the sixth century the Papacy became a conquering power. Under its direction missionaries proceeded beyond Gaul, to the very extremity of the ancient Empire, and converted the Anglo-Saxons, who had recently established themselves in Britain.   Here an ecclesiastical *provincia* was organized, as completely subject to the Bishop of Rome as the ancient political province had been to the Roman emperor.   From England missionaries went forth to preach the Christian faith in Germany, and, as one of its dogmas, obedience to the See of Rome.

Thus the Rome of St. Peter began her conquests where the Rome of Augustus had finished hers, in Britain and Germany.   These two countries are the first provinces of a Church Empire; they enter into history through the Church.   Hence it was the Papacy which first enlarged Europe.

§ 5. *Restoration of the Empire.*

Meanwhile, since the sixth century, Lombards and Greeks were contending for the possession of Italy.   Rome, which was menaced by the former, still belonged to the Emperor.   The Bishop of the Eternal City was thus the subject of the Byzantine βασιλεύς.   But Constantinople held out to him the prospect of nothing but insults, humiliations, and even dangers to the Christian faith. From the Lombards, likewise, he expected no good.   Between these two enemies he maintained

himself with difficulty. His secret desire was to
have Rome to himself; and this end he gradually attained by the very services that he rendered
in rebuilding her walls and in nourishing her people. He even dreamed of dominion over all Italy;
but he was still weak in the midst of violent enemies.

Watching carefully the course of events, he followed the progress of a new Frankish power.
For he, too, like the Gallo-Roman bishops of the
fifth century, was in quest of a people that might
become the workmen of God.

An Austrasian family, destined later to bear
the name of Carolingians, had recently acquired
great possessions between the Moselle and the
Rhine. In this family public office became hereditary. Its heads served the Merovingian crown as
mayors of the palace; but they were, in reality,
dukes of Austrasia, just as the Agilofings were
dukes of Bavaria. Their country was rich in men
of war, and was well situated to exert influence,
on the one hand, upon the German duchies and,
on the other, upon Neustria and Burgundy.

This country of the Rhine was, decidedly, the
principal theatre of history. There, on the con-
fines of the old world and the new, it was necessary
to live in order to become the controlling power
of the future. The Merovingian Franks left this
region too quickly, making Paris and Orléans their

favorite capitals.   They sank in the quicksands of
the Gallo-Roman population, and their energy was
prematurely stifled in the ashes of the past.   On
the other hand, the Franks of Austrasia, the Ripu-
arians of the Rhine, had preserved their primitive
energy, the practice of undertaking a campaign
every spring, and the love and enjoyment of war.

When the Merovingian Franks first appeared on
the scene, the Bishop of Rheims had been there
to greet them ; and ready to greet the Austrasian
Franks was the Bishop of Rome.   Being a greater
personage than St. Remi, the universal bishop proposed a higher task : with prayers and tears he
begged the Franks to constitute themselves the
protectors of the Apostle St. Peter.

The Franks did not at first understand this
proposition, and hesitated a long time.   Charles
Martel, intent on his work of war, did not trouble
himself to place his weapons at the service of a
priest.   But the priest insisted.   Pipin and Carlo-
man, sons of Charles, were already disciples of the
Church.   The latter died as a monk ; the former presided over ecclesiastical councils, and was zealous
in reforming the churches of Gaul and Germany.
When Pipin was elected king by the Franks, the
Pope went to Gaul to anoint him, just as Samuel
had anointed David.   Nevertheless, the alliance
was not final.   Charlemagne, son of Pipin, did not
come to an immediate understanding with the

Papacy.   For a time he was on good terms with
the Lombards, and chose a wife from among this
" most infamous tribe of lepers," as they were called
by the Holy Father.

Nevertheless, the spell exercised by the Church
continued to work, and became irresistible.   If
Charlemagne had been left to his own resources,
he would have had at his disposal only the power
and the ideas of a primitive king, that is to say, of
a military leader and a judge.   The Church nourished him with her learning—her theology, history,
literature, grammar, and astronomy.   She proposed
an ideal for his political and military activity, as
well as employment for his energy, by requesting
him "to defend the faith against the heretics
within, and to propagate it without over the lands
of the pagans."

To minds capable of reflection, Christianity
seemed at this time like a society of soldiers and
priests, governed by a soldier and a priest.   If
she could have forgotten the profane portion of
ancient history, she would have believed herself
again in biblical times, when the army fought on
the plain, and Moses prayed on the mountain.   This
figure is applicable to Charlemagne himself at a certain period of his reign.   But the traditions of profane antiquity thrust themselves upon the Bishop
of Rome and Charlemagne, and they agree to restore not the government of the people of God, but

the Roman Empire.   Thus in the year 800, in the basilica of St. Peter, Moses crowns Joshua, whom the Roman people salutes as Augustus.

§ 6. *The Historical World in the Year* 800.

The Pope claimed that he had established a single universal Emperor.   Ever since Odoacer had sent to Constantinople the imperial insignia, the Byzantine βασιλεύς had been " the sole master who sufficed for the world ; " but in the year 800 old Rome resumed her right to make emperors. Charlemagne was thus in theory the head of the world ; but Constantinople maintained against such a theory her actual possession of the imperial title, the legitimacy of which Charlemagne himself recognized.

These two empires would have embraced all Christianity, if the Anglo-Saxons in Britain, an independent Christian people, were not already entering upon a separate career of their own.   The Empire of the West, the Empire of the East, and England were the three political entities which at the beginning of the ninth century constituted Europe.

Outside of their boundaries were the infidels and the pagans.   The country of Islam—which was itself divided into an empire of the West, the caliphate of Cordova, and an empire of the East, the caliphate of Bagdad—extended, like a gigantic crescent, south of the two empires of which it was the common enemy. The pagans occupied all the North and East: Scandinavia, the immense, measureless region of Slavonia, and the country of the Avars.

Charlemagne destroyed the kingdom of the Avars on the Danube. He also conquered the Scandinavians and the Slavs of the Elbe; and, although he did not reduce them to subjection, he organized along his frontiers military counties or marches, which formed the vanguard of Christianity. He thus pointed out the way to his successors, and bequeathed to them the duty of waging war against the pagans and infidels.

§ 7. *Historical Effects of the Restoration of the Empire.*

The Empire of Charlemagne comprised certain ancient Christian countries which had obeyed Rome. These were: Gaul; Northern Spain, from the Pyrenees to the Ebro, taken from the Arabs; Italy, as far as the Garigliano, taken from the Lombards, a portion of which Pipin had given to the Pope as the patrimony of St. Peter; in addition, outside of the *orbis romanus*, Germany. Before the time of the Carolingians, Gaul, Italy, and Germany had each a separate existence. The Carolingians fused all these countries into the unity of the restored Empire.

This restoration is the great fact of the period, which is distinguished from that which precedes and from those which follow by a strange phenomenon: two ideal powers, the remembrance of pagan Rome and the authority of Christian Rome, were exclusively directing the material power of Western Europe.

The historian looks with more favor upon the new Rome, which subdued souls after having enlightened them, than upon ancient Rome, which conquered in order to dominate and to exploit. The conquest of Britain by a few Roman missionaries, armed only with the Cross, their chants, and their prayers, is certainly more admirable, more glorious, and more humane than the conquest by Agricola.

It is a source of pleasure to us also to consider the homage rendered by Charlemagne the Frank to the power of the past. This German is a descendant of the old enemies of Rome; in him is summed up, and, as it were, personified, the invasion of the barbarians which destroyed the Empire; and, to crown his victories, he restores the Empire. But the historian should not admire without reserve, unless he believes, as a sort of fatalistic optimist, that in this best of worlds everything has been for the best.

It is said that the Carolingian Empire had a

beneficial effect in preparing for the nations of the
future a common civilization—Christian, military,
and political; and that from this Empire were derived the typical Christian man of arms, and the
poetry of the conflict between the faithful of all
countries and the infidel. Would you eliminate
chivalry, the Crusades, and mediæval heroic poetry
from the history of sentiments and ideas?

No. But the nations of Europe on issuing from
their common cradle were to be hostile brothers.
After the vitality of the Carolingians had been exhausted, the West was again divided. There was as
much misery and bloodshed in destroying the edifice
as there had been in building it. The temporal
hegemony and the spiritual hegemony which the
Pope and Charlemagne had riveted together, col-
lided; and each of them, in turn, became tyrannical.
Are you so anxious to preserve in history the quarrel between the Papacy and the Empire, the oppression of Italy by Germany, and the long restraint
exercised on the human conscience by the Church?
Would you not gladly efface from the list of Crusades that against the Albigenses? When the
Pope consecrated Pipin, and when Charlemagne
and the Pope restored the Empire, they bequeathed
to future ages the coalition between the throne and
the altar. Do you not see the result, the whole
result?

It is not certain that without the alliance of the

Carolingians and the Papacy the Austrasian, the Aquitainian, the Lombard, the Bavarian, and the Saxon would have failed to find the standard of living that was best suited to each of them; that they would not have been just as fully permeated with the Christian spirit by adapting religion each to his own particular genius, as they did adapt it in later times.

Who knows? That is a question which one must frequently repeat. One thing appears certain: if the past is beneficent, because it initiates new generations into the experience of by-gone ages, it abuses its power. To the living some things in the past seem like impish pranks. One of these pranks was the re-establishment of the Empire, in the year 800, by a priest and a warrior, neither of whom knew exactly what the ancient Empire had been, and what the new one was to be.

CHAPTER III.

THE MIDDLE AGES.

§ 1. *General Characteristics.*

WE must first determine the limits and general characteristics of the period which is now to occupy our attention.

The Empire of the East maintained its existence like an agitated flame, sending forth great gleams of light, which vanished only to reappear with renewed brightness. During more than six centuries it defended itself against the darkness which finally overtook it.

The West began by undoing the work of the Carolingians; it broke up the Empire into kingdoms, and the kingdoms into feudal territories. A tangled and very rank vegetation thus obscured the general ideas of government. The imperial power, which lost a part of its authority every time it changed hands, and for which petty Italian princes contended, was reduced to a cipher; and the papal power, for which Roman fac-

tions contended, was debased. But in the middle
of the tenth century a Pope suddenly restored to
the Empire its lustre and strength by crowning as
Emperor, Otto, King of Germany.

These two powers then became the principal
factors in the politics of the West. In the pro-
tecting shadow of the Empire the Papacy was re-
invigorated and purified, and regained control over
the Church, which was once more losing itself
in worldly cares and obligations. Having become
the head of an immense spiritual army, the Papacy constrained the Empire at first to respect her
independence, and soon afterward to recognize
her primacy of rank.

If these two powers had acted in harmony they
would have been mistresses of the West, where
they would have long prevented national development. In fact, the Papacy did not desire to hear
anything concerning quarrels between nations. In
her eyes only one kind of war was legitimate and
perpetually obligatory, namely, war against the
infidel, and, by way of interlude, war against the
heretic and the excommunicate. In order that
Christians might perform the duty of waging this
war of God, the Pope tried to impose upon them
the peace of God. Whoever interfered with this
peace, whether a petty baron or a Henry of England, a Philip of France, or an Emperor Frederick, was a rebel.

Thus the Crusades formed the principal phenomenon of political history in the twelfth and thirteenth centuries; but they quickly miscarried, and finally failed lamentably. The kings turned away from this ruinous undertaking. Other interests attracted their attention, undertakings nearer home and more lucrative. National territories began to appear, and the nations began to be conscious of the fact that they possessed a frontier.

The two leading powers were themselves the cause of their own destruction. The Papacy ruined the Empire in the thirteenth century; but she soon met with resistance from the kings, who had become heads of nations, and she fell into the scandals of the Great Schism.

Thus from the wreck of the two universal powers the various nationalities emerged. Just as Christianity had succeeded the Roman Empire, so Europe succeeded Christianity. But how confused and chaotic Europe still was! It is, therefore, necessary to look further for a date of demarcation in the political history of the Continent. In the fourteenth century the veritable Middle Ages came to a close. But there was still an Empire of the East, which even seemed to be animated with new life; there was still a Holy Empire, which even did its utmost to perform its duties as protector of the Church during the disorders of the Great Schism; and there still survived the illusion and even the heroic enterprises of the Crusades.   In the fifteenth century the Schism and the Mussulman still preoccupy and trouble Joan of Arc.   In the interval between two battles the knights of the West vow on the pheasant the extermination of the infidel.

Nevertheless, the infidel captured Constantinople.   Europe, which had sought combats with him in his own country, permitted the Turk to transform the patriarchal church of St. Sophia into a mosque.   Europe left to the petty states of the Balkan Peninsula the task of stopping the Asiatic on the road that led to the heart of the Continent.   The most Christian King of France, the Catholic King of Spain, and the Pope himself weighed the price of an alliance with the Ottomans, and allowed such an alliance to enter as an element in their political calculations—a sure indication that a period in the history of Europe is concluded.

Thus it is now necessary for us to trace the history of the various countries of the West and the East from the time of Charlemagne to about the end of the fifteenth century.

§ 2. *The Empire of the East.*

During this long period the contrast between the West and the East became more and more marked.

The Empire in the West was a power almost
ideal, without a fixed territory, without even a
name, for the periphrase by which it was desig-
nated, "the Holy Roman Empire of the German
Nation," was not a name. The Empire in the
East was a real sovereignty, exercised over a defi-
nite region, and bearing a national name, that of
"Romania."

The Empire in the West was divided into two
powers—one spiritual, the other temporal. In the
East the Empire did not tolerate by its side a sacerdotal monarchy, independent of the civil power.
The βασιλεύς was a sort of pope-king. At the
very time when the Papacy, having become all-
powerful, ruled over the kings of the West, the
schism separated Constantinople from Rome.

The Byzantine Empire was thus more coherent
and stronger than its rival. But it had to cope
with three distinct enemies: an internal enemy
consisting of ethnographical groups, which were
established on its territory, but which it had not
assimilated ; and two external enemies, the Catholic West and the Moslem East.

A threefold question presented itself concerning
the destiny of this Empire. Would the nations
established within its territory remain in possession
of it, and the Balkan Peninsula be divided, already
in the Middle Ages, into petty independent states?
Would the West seize Constantinople and the

Balkan Peninsula? Or, perchance, would Constantinople and the Peninsula become the prey of Asia?

The time arrived when the nations of the Balkan Peninsula were successful. In the ninth century Bulgaria became a powerful state, and Slavic principalities were established; in the fourteenth century Servia was an empire.

At one time the West regarded itself as master of the East. Papal and knightly Europe had undertaken the Crusades to regain from the infidels the holy places wrested from the βασιλεύς. For this purpose many thousands of men had been sent to Asia. The Emperor of the East, who was much superior to these barbarians in politics, had deceived them. He had recovered, by means of the first Crusades, parts of Asia Minor which his empire had lost. But the merchants of Venice also were statesmen. Circumstances gave them the direction of the Fourth Crusade; and the Christian barons, who were as covetous as the Republic of the Lagunes, divided the Empire in the beginning of the thirteenth century. Thus there ruled at Constantinople a Flemish emperor; at Thessalonica, an Italian king; in Achaia, at Naxos, and at Athens, petty dynasties; while Venice took possession of Crete and the Peloponnesus.

As to the Asiatic, the third of the possible conquerors of the Byzantine Empire, he constantly attacked the latter. After the Arab Empire, which included Asia, Africa, Spain, and Sicily, had fallen, the Ottoman emir in Asia became a formidable neighbor.

Against all these enemies the βασιλεύς defended himself with a constancy and skill that compel admiration. Such was the vitality of the "sick man" of this time that he recovered from the strange catastrophe of the Fourth Crusade. At the close of the thirteenth century he reconquered Constantinople. The Empire, thus restored, recommenced the conquest of the Peninsula; it regained its three seas, and pushed its dominion to the Peloponnesus. It seemed to be strong enough to prevail over the Slavs, the Bulgarians, the principalities of Epirus, Achaia, and Athens, and over Venice. But the power of the Turks in Asia grew stronger and stronger.

In Asia there was a great reserve of men and soldiers, led by a dynasty of absolute chiefs, who all desired one and the same thing. The great conflict between these Turks and the Byzantine Empire is conspicuous in the history of the fourteenth and fifteenth centuries. Finally Constantinople became the capital of the Ottoman state, which embraced the whole peninsula from the Save to Cape Matapan, excepting the heroic Montenegro, and certain points that remained Venetian.

Thus Asia took revenge on Europe for the Persian Wars, and for the conquests of Alexander, the Romans, the Byzantine Emperor, and the crusaders. She was destined to extend her empire in the Mediterranean by the conquest of certain islands and of Africa, and toward central Europe by the progress of the Turks along the Danube. In this condition the Eastern Question was to remain a long time; Slavs, Bulgarians, Albanians, Roumanians, and Greeks slept under the sway of the scimitar and the crescent; but they only slept.

§ 3. *The Empire of the West.*

After the death of Charlemagne the ecclesiastical and imperialist party tried in vain to maintain the unity of the Empire. The force of circumstances, permanently felt amid the accidents of politics and chance, had separated Germany, France, and Italy; but the separation, begun with the Treaty of Verdun in 843, was not complete.

These three countries were not states, for a state is an organized political entity; there were no states, properly speaking (at least no great states), before the close of the Middle Ages. Nor were they nations; a nation is a definitely formed, conscious, and responsible person; there were no real nations on the Continent before our own times.

In the ninth century France and Germany had
not yet received their names.   Charles the Bald
was king of the Franks; Lewis the German was
also king of the Franks.   They were distinguished
by the points of the compass.   Charles ruled over
" the Western Franks," Lewis over "the Eastern
Franks."   Gradually and very slowly each of the
two countries worked out its own destiny.

As for Germany and Italy, they were bound
together by the restoration of the Empire in the
tenth century.   Thenceforth the same personage
was at once king in Germany, king in Italy, and
Emperor.   Germany and Italy were the habitation
of the priesthood and of the Empire—an honor of
considerable and prolonged consequence for the
future of both countries.

§ 4. *Empire and Church—Consequences for Germany.*

In the Middle Ages the most active man in the
world, and the most singular political personage,
was the Emperor-King.   He did not succeed in gaining recognition as a universal monarch, and did
not even become the monarch of any one nation.
Not knowing what name to assume, he called himself briefly *imperator.*   His legal capital was Rome,
but he did not reside there.   He had no capital in
Germany.   He had, in fact, no fixed habitation.

In the period of Carolingian decadence the cus-

tom of electing kings had been regularly established. Thus it was necessary to be elected in
order to become king of Germany. On the other
hand, to become Emperor the person elected king
had to be crowned by the Pope at Rome. If the
German king had been simply a king, he would
doubtless have been able to dispense with the election, as the Capetians did in France after the fifth
royal generation. But he was at the same time
Emperor; and the Pope never admitted that the
imperial dignity was hereditary, or that the coronation was to be considered a vain formality. The
Pope combined with the German princes to per-
petuate the custom of election, which placed the
elect at the mercy of the electors, and obliged him
to make terms with the Bishop of Rome. Hence
in Germany there was not the continuity of monarchical policy that transformed other countries
into states, which afterward became nations.

The clearest function of the Emperor being his
protectorship of the Church, he had to look after the welfare of the Papacy, and raise it from
the disgraceful condition into which it had fallen
in the tenth century; then, after having given it
strength enough to combat with him, he found it
necessary to combat with it. As protector of the
Church and as king of Italy, he was entangled in
all the affairs of the Peninsula, where he found
allies and also enemies.

As for Germany, she was one of the theatres of the conflict between the Emperor and the Pope. Not merely the ecclesiastical, but also the secular princes, favoring the disorder which increased their independence, sided with the Pope against the Emperor.

From the middle of the thirteenth century Germany was merely an anarchical federation of principalities and republics. There was no longer any collective national life, no national army, finance, or judiciary. Everywhere war prevailed, and there was no longer any law save that of the fist (*Faustrecht*). To protect themselves, princes and cities formed leagues for the maintenance of peace; these leagues themselves were militant, for they waged war to prevent war.

Over this disorder a monarch presided who still called himself Emperor. But at the close of the thirteenth century, under the trappings of this title, he was only a petty German prince, exploiting his high office to make the fortune of his house. Thus the Luxemburgs, poor squires of the country of Ardennes, and the Hapsburgs, small seigneurs of the country of Argovia, secured a family domain. "Everyone for himself" was the motto of Germany at this time. Hence the country which in the tenth century seemed to be nearer to unity than any other Carolingian land, sank into anarchy.

§ 5. *Consequences for Italy.*

Italy was no more predestined to be divided
than Germany. The fact that we were long accustomed to see these two countries divided, leads
one to think that they followed their natural bent;
but there is nothing to prove that unity was more
difficult to establish in Germany and Italy than in
other regions. Without doubt their geography
places obstacles in the way of unity; but are not
such obstacles also to be found in Spain, and even
in France? In fact, the great divergence between
the destinies of France and Germany, or Spain and
Italy, has been created by history.

In France a Germanic people, the Franks—
established on Gallo-Roman soil, mingling their
blood, spirit, and laws with the blood, spirit, and
laws of the ancient population—became the artisan of a new nationality. In Italy this same end
could have been attained, first by the Ostrogoths,
and afterward by the Lombards. The Papacy,
however, considered them as strangers and enemies. When the Lombards were on the point of
occupying Rome, the Pope summoned the Franks.
In Northern Italy Charlemagne superseded the
king whom he had conquered; but in the South
he left in existence Lombard duchies, and countries
under the Byzantine dominion. He and Pipin

founded a papal state. These southern duchies, the principality of St. Peter, and the kingdom of the north mark the beginning of Italian polyarchy.

The Empire having apparently sunk in the shipwreck of the Carolingian family, attempts were made to found an Italian monarchy. But the Pope terminated them by restoring the Empire; and he placed the Peninsula under the Teutonic yoke, which was so odious to the Italians, and which was perpetuated in divers forms to our day.

The Papacy inaugurated a formidable game by opposing barbarians against barbarians. To drive the German Hohenstaufens from the kingdom of the Two Sicilies, a Pope, in the second half of the thirteenth century, summoned the Angevins of France.

It would be displaying lack of intelligence to accuse the mediæval Papacy of offending against an Italian nationality, which had no existence. The Pope could be neither the vassal of a city nor the vassal of a country without forfeiting some of his dignity, which was the highest in the world. It was his defined function or office to adopt a universal policy; and he sought thereby to guarantee the independence and power of the See of the Apostles. At the close of the Middle Ages he became an Italian prince, and adopted an Italian policy; but this compromised the Papacy, and even the Church.

Nevertheless, Machiavelli, considering the matter from an Italian point of view, was right in at-
tributing to the Popes the disorganization of Italy,
to which they at least largely contributed.

As in Germany, so in Italy, at first, from the
tenth to the thirteenth century, feudal principalities and republics were established; then, from the
middle of the thirteenth century to the end of the
Middle Ages, most of the republics were transformed into principalities. In the fifteenth century Milan, Florence, the Papal State, the oli-
garchic republic of Venice, and the kingdom of
Naples formed a pentarchy, each of them looking
after its own separate interests, and none of them
acquainted with the sentiment of Italian patriotism.

§ 6. *Expansion of Italy.*

Anarchy in Germany and polyarchy in Italy
do not mean that Germany and Italy were inert.
Not having a common master, nor a common life,
nor collective patriotism, these countries suffered
the evils of constant civil war. Moreover, in modern times they became the battle-fields of European
politics. But there is some compensation in not
having a government which employs all its powers
in a well-defined policy. Italy was broken in fragments, but lived a life all the more intense, because
it was in conformity with the natural aptitudes of

each section.　If an Italian monarchy had had its seat at Rome, Rome would have lost its incomparable originality as a sacerdotal and universal city, and history would not have known of Florentine or Venetian energy.

Already the Renaissance had begun.　It was a natural product of the classical Italian soil, but polyarchy favored its development, and permitted its free and varied growth.　While waiting for the Italian spirit to expand over all Europe, the great Italian cities ruled the Mediterranean.　They formed the medium of communication between the Orient and the Occident, and thus rapidly grew rich.　They invented and perfected commercial institutions, such as the consulate, exchange, and the bank.　The bankers of France were called Lombards ; and Italian money was current throughout all Western Europe, where people reckoned by ducats, the money of the two dogal towns, Genoa and Venice, and by florins, on which was impressed the flower of Florence.

There was something like a Mediterranean empire of Italy.　For Genoa possessed Corsica and Sardinia, and Venice owned a large part of the Adriatic coast and many of the islands of the Archipelago.　In fact, before the arrival of the Turks Venice ruled over three-eighths of the old Greek Empire.

§ 7. *Expansion of Germany in the North and East—The Three Zones.*

German anarchy in the Middle Ages was very energetic and fruitful.

Carolingian Germany was almost comprised in the country situated between the Rhine and the Elbe. It was capable of expansion in three directions: toward the south natural highways, extending over the mountains, led invitingly into Italy; on the west, between France and Germany, lay a region—bounded by the Rhine and the Meuse, the Rhone and the Alps—whose political destiny was uncertain, for it was exposed to the competition of the two nations; and on the north and east an immense, undefined stretch of territory was open to German colonization.

It was official or imperial Germany which interfered in Italy, where, with a few rare exceptions, she wrought mischief. In the west Germanic activity was early impeded, then arrested, by France. In a large part of the third region Germany succeeded in securing a foothold.

The northern and eastern frontier of Germany was in Carolingian times that of Christianity. To extend this frontier, and keep extending it, until the last pagan submitted, was converted, and became the faithful subject of both Pope and Em-

peror, was the necessary foreign policy or function of the Empire, which had been restored the
first time in the year 800, and a second time in
962.

In Charlemagne's time a multitude of pagan
and barbarian tribes were ranged in echelons
along the Christian frontier, and they extended
into the unknown region of the European Far-
East and into the peninsula of the north.

At the mouths of the Elbe were the Scandinavians; all along the Elbe and the Saale, from the
shores of the Baltic to the mountains of Bohemia,
were the Slavic Polabi; in Bohemia, the Slavic
Tsechs; on the Danube, Turanian hordes of
Avars, who were afterward displaced by the Mag-
yars; and in the southeast, as far as the Adriatic, other Slavic tribes. Behind this first zone of
tribes, with most of which Charlemagne had come
in contact, a second, entirely Slavic, extended from
north to south, comprising Pomerania, Poland,
and Silesia. Still farther away, along the eastern
Baltic, lived Finns and Lithuanians; and in the
great plain beyond them, the Russians.

The task of bringing all these tribes within the
bounds of Christian civilization should have been
divided between the Empires of the East and
West. But the Empire of the East could barely
defend its own life, and the Empire of the West
united the forces of Germany under its command

during only a very short time. Hence the Christianizing and civilizing work was performed almost entirely by private enterprise.

§ 8. *Progress of Germany in the First Zone.*

From the Scandinavians Germany won nothing. The three kingdoms—Denmark, Sweden, and Norway — were established and Christianized in the tenth century. But to be Christianized meant to acquire the right to live. Every time that a people entered the Church, the Europe of the future was enriched by a new recruit. Denmark, a neighbor of the Empire, had relations with the latter; and at times her king was a sort of vassal of the Emperor; but her ordinary status was one of independence. The Scandinavian kings were soon able to contend with the Germans for the possession of the Baltic, that sombre Mediterranean upon which were fought so many obscure and violent battles between competing tribes.

On the other hand, Germany extended her boundaries very quickly in the region of the Slavs of the Elbe, where she ever afterward retained her dominion. At the close of the twelfth century the Slavs of the country between the Saale and the Elbe were Germanized and converted to Christianity. This was the work of the margraves of

Lusatia and Misnia. The Slavs of the country between the Elbe and the Oder were in great part exterminated. This was the work of the dukes of Saxony and of "the Margraves of the North," who in the twelfth century assumed the name of Margraves of Brandenburg, a name destined to become celebrated. The Slavs of the shores of the Baltic received throngs of colonists; their princes were Germanized, and their country, Mecklenburg, became a trans-Elbine prolongation of Lower Germany. Thus the whole northern part of the first zone was acquired by Germany.

The Tsechs in Bohemia defended themselves more successfully; their dukes became kings and Christians, which circumstance saved them. It is true that they were vassals of the Emperor; and the crown of Bohemia, which was elective, was finally attached to the head of German princes, the Hapsburgs. But the destiny of the Tsechs was very different from that of the Slavs of the North. They preserved their race, language, and peculiar genius. Hence there is a Tsech question in Austria at the present day. There is no Polabian question, because the Polabi have disappeared.

§ 9. *Progress of Germany in the Second Zone.*

The Germans naturally made less progress in the zone of the Oder. Pomerania, Poland, and Silesia received crowds of German colonists—husbandmen, merchants, artisans, and soldiers. But the duchy of Pomerania maintained an indigenous dynasty until the seventeenth century; and the Germans in this country encountered the competition of the Scandinavians. Silesia, which broke up into duchies and principalities, belonged to no one ruler.

Already in the Middle Ages Poland was preparing the way for the disasters of the future. She allowed Pomerania to escape from her grasp, a country which would have given her a seaboard; and also Silesia, whose mountains would have sheltered her. She remained a kingdom wholly exposed on every side. She did not succeed in securing consolidation or organization. Her feudal cavalry while on the gallop made conquests which she did not preserve. She was not able to produce a royal race, and her elective crown was open to the competition of foreign families. Nevertheless, Poland was a Slavic Christian kingdom, more independent than Bohemia. Germany, which in the north encountered a Scandinavia, met with a Slavonia in the east. The Europe of the future became more complicated in proportion to its expansion.

4

§ 10. *Progress of Germany in the Third Zone.*

Germany penetrated as far as the third zone. Here the Finns were peopling Finland, and were advancing along the coasts of Livonia and Esthonia. Next to them, on the south, came various Indo-European tribes—Lithuanians, Lettes, and Prussians—extending from the interior of Livonia to the mouth of the Vistula. Inimical to each other, pagans, still remaining in the impotent state of primitive barbarism, these tribes of the eastern Baltic, while awaiting the still far-distant awakening of Russia, were the prey of the nations of the West. Sweden took possession of Finland and Carelia; Denmark secured Esthonia. But the greatest acquisitions were made by the Germans.

The Hanse, a league of German merchants who were, after their fashion, both soldiers and crusaders, covered the shores of the Baltic with their federated emporiums. A knightly German order, that of the Sword-bearers, was founded even at Riga. Another, that of the Teutonic Knights, started in Palestine, and there had a brilliant career; then, after having been exiled from the Holy Land, it established itself in Prussia. Knowing how to conquer and to govern, it founded a state which is one of the curiosities of history. The two orders, having united under one grand-master

in the second half of the thirteenth century,
ruled over a vast and rich country.   Its two
principal provinces, Livonia and Prussia, filled
with German colonists, were like an exterior Germany, a German vanguard in the European Far-
East.   In the north, this dominion extended as
far as the Narva; on the south, a series of conquests, made at the expense of Pomerania and
Poland, placed the German Knights in communication with the German margraves of Brandenburg.

§ 11. *Progress of Germany in the Valley of the Danube.*

Southeast of Germany, in the valley of the
Danube, the path of expansion was narrower than
in the north, and more difficult.   The valley of
the river contracts between the projecting mountains of Bohemia and those of the Alps.   Moreover, Bavaria could not furnish a contingent of
emigrants so large as that of North Germany,
with her great plain and immense seaboard.

At the point where the Danube valley widens,
the Hungarian horde finally fixed its permanent en-
campment.   Like the Danes, Bohemians, and Poles,
the Hungarians entered the history of Europe on
the day when they were converted to Christianity.
They had relations with the Empire, but they rec-

ognized its suzerainty only a short time. Their elective crown, like that of the Bohemians, became permanently attached to the heads of the Hapsburgs. But the Hungarian remained Hungarian, even more than the Tsech remained Tsech. Hence there is at the present day an Hungarian question, as there is a Tsech question; and the Hapsburg whose function it is to solve both, will solve neither.

§ 12. *Résumé of the Expansion of Germany.*

Thus Germany diffused abroad her superfluous strength. All classes of her population competed in the conquest, colonization, and development of an immense tract of country. The princes of the frontier conquered the border-lands. The knights recruited the two orders (Teutonic Knights and Sword-bearers), and assisted them in their conflicts with the indigenous population by crusades, incessantly renewed. The regular and secular clergy sent missionaries, monks, priests, and bishops. The merchants built new cities, or transformed into cities various villages along the coast of the Baltic and along the river banks. The tool of the German artisan and the plough of the German peasant brought riches where barbarism had prevailed. The allurement of adventures, the spirit of religious proselytism, the hope of gain or of martyrdom, the love of independence, the search for liberty and property, attracted these various categories of emigrants to this America. And Germany, which stopped at the Elbe in Carolingian times, now extended to the Niemen. She had subjugated or destroyed many enemies of the Christian world, those that Charlemagne had known and fought, and others whose very names he had never heard.

In the fifteenth century, it is true, the fortune of the Germans declined. Two formidable enemies appeared simultaneously: the Turks, who eventually conquered almost the whole of Hungary, and menaced the German possessions on the Danube; and Poland, which took the offensive against the Germans, after her union with Lithuania, the great unconquered enemy of the Teutonic Knights. Poland dismembered the principality of the Knights, took from them the mouths of the Vistula, and made Dantzig a royal Polish city; thus communication was cut off between Germany and the Order—between the main body of the army and the vanguard, which was now placed in a very perilous position. But the Turkish power was to remain barbarian and Asiatic; and Poland was incapable of acquiring the solidity of a well-regulated state. The centuries that followed were to witness the revenge of Germany on Slav and Turk.

§ 13. *Effects of this Expansion on German History—Austria and Prussia*

This development of German power is not merely a great event in the history of Europe; its effects on Germany herself were very important. On the disputed frontier, in the zone of perpetual conflict, were formed and developed the two states which, in turn, were to dominate over Germany, namely, Austria and Prussia. Both were born in the midst of the enemy.

The cradle of Austria was the Eastern march, established by Charlemagne on the Danube, beyond Bavaria, at the very gate through which have passed so many invaders from the Orient. It was a veritable field of battle of the German race, lying between Slavic Bohemia and Carinthia, and confronted first by the Avar, then by the Hungarian. Since the end of the thirteenth century it belonged to the Hapsburgs. They also acquired, successively, the ancient march of Carinthia, the county of Tyrol, and Trieste. These acquisitions, together with the march of Austria, formed a group of provinces, half German, half Slavic, which extended to the Adriatic and Italy, and had necessarily relations with two kingdoms of the Eastern zone, namely, Bohemia and Hungary. Already, in the fifteenth century, a Hapsburg of

Austria was king of these two countries, an index and a presage of the future. Two centuries earlier the imperial crown had already been worn by a Hapsburg; and since the fifteenth century, although still elective in theory, it was in practice hereditary in the Austrian house. This was another factor in the future destiny of the Hapsburgs. At the end of the Middle Ages they were merely poor princes, but they were about to become the foremost monarchs in the world.

The cradle of Prussia was the march of Brandenburg, between the Elbe and the Oder, in the region of the exterminated Slavs. It was a poor country, quite flat, and swept by winds, which heaped up the sands in barren hills. By persistent effort this march conquered the right to exist. It had already survived many catastrophes, when, at the beginning of the fifteenth century, it became the property of the Hohenzollerns. Brandenburg had to choose between the alternatives of increasing in extent (for a fatherland cannot be constructed out of a morsel of plain) or of perishing. It increased toward the ocean, to the detriment of Mecklenburg and Pomerania; and also toward the mountains, across Lusatia and Silesia. It was the great German champion of the Northeast, the collaborator of the Teutonic Knights, with whom, at the end of the fourteenth century, it desired to divide Poland.

This harmony between the margraves and the Teutonic Order, and this similarity of vocation, presaged the future. The time was near at hand when the Prussia of the Teutonic Knights was to be united to the march of Brandenburg by an indissoluble bond. Then the Brandenburg-Prussian state was to proclaim itself the heir of the knights, priests, merchants, and peasants who had been the pioneers of Germanism beyond the Elbe.

§ 14. *The Intermediate Region between Germany and France.*

In striking contrast with the enormous advance of Germany in the East was the decline of her power in the West.

The history of the region between Germany and France is very singular. When the three sons of Lewis the Pious divided the Empire in the ninth century, they found it very natural to give the Emperor Lothair both Rome and Aix-la-Chapelle, the two imperial capitals; for the men of that time had no sense of the reality of things, but followed blindly the ideas that possessed their minds. Hence Lothair received Italy and a long strip of territory between the Scheldt, the Meuse, and the Rhone, on the one side, and the Rhine and the Alps, on the other. Thus there was placed between the future Germany and the future France a field of combat, which has already witnessed, and doubtless will again witness, many battles.

This long and narrow strip was soon divided into two portions : Burgundy, between the Alps, the Saone, the Rhone, and the Mediterranean; and Lorraine, to the north of Burgundy. As Germany was at first much stronger than France, she dominated both regions; and Lorraine and Burgundy became countries of the Empire. But the imperial power grew weaker just when the kingdom of France was growing stronger. Furthermore, Germany was not well protected along the western frontier; nor did she here come in contact with pagans, as in the East. The frontier, moreover, was not sharply defined by a difference of language, race, and civilization. Nor were there on this frontier any German states organized for war. While margraves guarded the course of the Elbe, the Rhine became " the highway of the priests." German energy, so conspicuous in the East, languished in these principalities of archbishops, bishops, and abbots. By the close of the fifteenth century the Empire had lost almost all its western dependencies, while France was gaining ground in this territory.

§ 15. *Formation of France.*

When France was detached from the Empire, in the ninth century, of all three imperial regions she was the one which seemed least likely to form a nation. There was no unity in the country west of the Scheldt, the Meuse, and the Rhone. Various principalities, duchies, or counties were here formed, but each of them was divided into secular fiefs and ecclesiastical territories.

Over these fiefs and territories the authority of the duke or the count, which was supposed to represent that of the king, was exercised only in case these seigneurs had sufficient power, derived from their own personal estates.

Destitute of domains and almost starving, the king, in official documents, asked what means he might find on which to live with some degree of decency. From time to time, amid this chaos, he discussed the theory of his authority. He was a lean and solemn phantom, straying about among living men who were very rude and energetic. The phantom kept constantly growing leaner, but royalty did not vanish. People were accustomed to its existence, and the men of those days could not conceive of a revolution. By the election of Hugh Capet, in 987, royalty became a reality, because the king, as Duke of *Francia*, had lands, money, and followers.

It would be out of place to seek a plan of conduct and a methodical line of policy in the actions of the Capetians, for they employed simultaneously every sort of expedient.

During more than three centuries they had male offspring; thus the chief merit of the dynasty was that it endured. As always happens, out of the practice developed a law; and this happy accident produced a lawful hereditary succession, which was a great element of strength.

Moreover, the king had a whole arsenal of rights: old rights of Carolingian royalty, preserving the remembrance of imperial power, which the study of the Roman law was soon to resuscitate, transforming these apparitions into formidable realities; old rights conferred by the coronation, which were impossible to define, and hence incontestable; and rights of suzerainty, newer and more real, which were definitely determined and codified as feudalism developed, and which, joined to the other rights mentioned above, made the king proprietor of France.

These are the elements that Capetian royalty contributed to the play of fortuitous circumstances. Everything turned to its profit: the miseries of the Church, which, unarmed in the midst of a violent society, claimed the royal protection from one end of the kingdom to the other; and also the efforts of the middle classes to be admitted with well-defined rights into feudal society (for the king, the head of this society, was the natural protector of these new-comers, the burgesses of the French towns). His authority was thus exercised, outside the limits of his own particular domain, throughout the whole kingdom. He did more: he gradually united France to his domain. He acquired petty principalities, such as the counties of Amiens, Vermandois, and Valois. By rightful authority and by force he took possession of Normandy, Anjou, Maine, Touraine, and Poitou. This conquest, which the wicked imbecility of John of England facilitated, insured the success of the Capetians. From that time onward water poured from all directions into the great central stream. When, in the war against the Albigenses, the Church and the knights of the North destroyed a feudal dynasty and a separate civilization, the king acquired Languedoc. When Philip the Fair, by marriage, gained Champagne, the domain of the king extended to the imperial frontier as well as to the Mediterranean and the ocean.

§ 16. *Expansion of France.*

In the eleventh and twelfth centuries, while royalty was still very weak and anarchy prevailed in the kingdom, France, like Italy and Germany, diffused abroad her vital energy. Unfortunately she had not within reach, like Germany, an undefined region inhabited by barbarians and pagans, that is to say, reputed to be without an owner and open to Christian occupancy. France threw herself, so to speak, into the Crusades; she charged herself with " deeds of God " against the infidel.. She gave kings to Jerusalem and Cyprus, dukes to Athens, and emperors to Constantinople. She built upon this holy illusion of Christianity, not without profit to her fame, that fame which she early began to love as a patrimony.

Knights of France also founded a Christian kingdom in Portugal, upon soil which was then Moslem; others wrested South Italy from the Saracens and Greeks; but neither the kingdom of Portugal nor the kingdom of the Two Sicilies became French territory.

The expansion of France in Europe during the Middle Ages was pre-eminently intellectual. Her intellect gave expression to the whole civilization of that period—religious, feudal, and knightly. The French wrote heroic poems, built castles and cathedrals, and interpreted the texts of Aristotle and the Scriptures. Their songs, buildings, and scholastic philosophy verged upon perfection. Already independent, already mobile and sprightly, the French mind freed itself from tradition and authority. It produced the aërial grace of Gothic art. It parodied its own heroic songs, and sculptured caricatures on the walls of its monuments of religion. It gave as companion to " Monsieur Saint Louis," who lived in heaven, Sire de Joinville, who loved the earth, especially his lands and his fine castle of Champagne ; he avoided the sight of these possessions when he went on the Crusade, lest tears should fill his eyes, which were not prone to weep. The French mind produced prose—French prose—as well as poetry. Among the theologians it almost produced philosophers.

Christian Europe copied French cathedrals, recited French heroic and humorous songs, and thus learned the French language. Foreigners spoke French " because the tongue of France was more delectable, and common to all people." Among the Masters of Arts in the Christian world the most erudite were those who had successfully defended a thesis at the University of Paris. Almost all the universities of Europe were like swarms of bees from the hive on Mount St. Geneviève. A proverb said that the world was ruled by three powers—the Papacy, the Empire, and Learning ; the first residing in Rome, the second in Germany, the third in Paris.

Political history cannot neglect these facts of intellectual progress. In other countries other forms of genius have been characterized by power and beauty. None has been as radiant as that of

France. The light which she diffused throughout Christendom contributed to the formation of Europe, by creating resemblances between widely different nations. In the Middle Ages this was the way in which the French worked for the welfare of others.

§17. *The Royal Policy—French Patriotism.*

Soon the age of adventure in France came to a close, and French energy was absorbed by the royal policy. The French monarchs, from the time when they began to take possession of the kingdom, had had a policy. They were entangled by family interests in the affairs of Italy, and, consequently, in those of Aragon; but these were merely accidental circumstances. Toward England, on the other hand, they were compelled to adopt a watchful and permanent policy.

In 1066 a vassal of the French king, William, Duke of Normandy, conquered England, and became more potent than his feudal lord. His successors, by fortunate alliances, greatly increased their French domain, which at one time included the whole of the Atlantic seaboard of France. Hence war with England was a necessity.

At first this was a feudal war between vassal and lord, men of the same country, who spoke the same language. At the beginning of the fourteenth century, the direct line of the Capetians died out, and the crown of France was contested by two French princes, one of whom was King Edward of England, and the other, Philip of Valois. The war which broke out was not a conflict between one nation and another, between the genius of one people and that of another; nevertheless, it continued, and was fierce as well as long. From year to year the hatred against the English increased. In contact with the foreigner, France began to know herself, like the *ego* in contact with the *non-ego*. Vanquished, she felt the disgrace of defeat. Acts of municipal and local patriotism preceded and heralded French patriotism, which finally blossomed out in Joan of Arc, and sanctified itself with the perfume of a miracle. Out of France with the English! They left France, and France came into existence.

She existed at first in and through the king, who, in his living flesh and in his privileged blood, personified the idea, still too abstract, of a native country. War itself, with its cortege of misery and ruin, made royalty all-powerful. War mowed down the nobility, bankrupted the municipalities, and weakened all the powers of resistance. It permitted the king, the defender of the country, to decree general measures, to make laws, to provide himself with a royal army, royal finances, and a royal administration. In a word, it per-

fected the French monarchy, which at the close
of the fifteenth century was one of the greatest
powers in Europe—in fact, the greatest.

§ 18. *Progress of France in the Intermediate Region.*

Let us now return to the intermediate region
between Germany and France. While Germany
coped with the East, and France with the West,
the regions of Burgundy and Lorraine, not having
in themselves a sufficient reason for independent
existence, and not knowing what they ought to become, sank into inextricable disorder.

Burgundy began to fall to pieces at the very
time when the German emperors were wearing the
crown of Arles. In the thirteenth century there
was no longer a separate king of Arles, no royal
titulary to represent the Burgundian kingdom in
dealings with foreign countries. At this very
juncture the crusade against the Albigenses exposed the South to the armies and state-craft of the
Capetians. One of the consequences of this event
was that a Capetian prince acquired the marqui-
sate of Provence. In the fourteenth century Lyons and the Dauphiné were added to the royal
domain; and in the fifteenth century Provence
became the immediate possession of the crown.
Thus, at the end of the Middle Ages, the list of

5

French cities included Lyons—the great Roman city, which had been the sanctuary of the worship of Augustus, and had become the seat of the primate of Gaul—Arles, likewise a Roman city, afterward the capital of the kingdom of Burgundy, and Marseilles, the oldest city in Gaul.

An accident—the conquest of England by the Normans—had confined the efforts of the Capetians to the West; another accident, the crusade against the Albigenses, had attracted their activity to the south of the Burgundian region, far from their proper sphere of action. Here work of a confused nature, singular experiments, were in progress: the Swiss Confederation and Savoy were beginning to take form.

The Swiss Confederation was born in Swabia, at the southwest extremity of Germany. Its first additions were made in Swabia and Italy; but toward the close of the fifteenth century it began to expand in the upper valley of the Rhone. It lost its Germanic character, to become something very distinct and peculiar, a league of peasants and cities grouped in cantons, expanding little by little despite obstacles of nature and racial differences within its bounds.

The state of Savoy was born on the frontier of Burgundy and Italy. It seemed at first as though it would develop on Burgundian soil. The counts of Maurienne, having become counts, then dukes,

of Savoy, were important personages on that side
of the mountains.   But the progress of France
and of the Swiss leagues soon held them in check,
and drove them toward Italy.   The first duke of
Savoy was also prince of Piedmont.   The formation of a state, at once cisalpine and transalpine, .
was a harbinger of the future.

§ 19. *The House of Burgundy.*

The destiny of the Lorraine region was also
uncertain.   Here there was a confused state of
things : countries without a ruler, like Alsace ;
principalities like the duchy which retained and
perpetuated the name of Lorraine, and like the
duchies and counties of the Netherlands ; and
ecclesiastical feudal lordships, like the bishopric of
Liège.   In the midst of this feudal régime without an effective lord, the cities—surrounded by
nobles who lived by war — were nurseries of industry and the greatest commercial centres of
Europe.

An attempt was made by the dukes of Burgundy, princes of the house of France, to reunite
under one government the regions of Burgundy
and Lorraine.

The duchy of Burgundy was wholly outside the
ancient kingdom of Burgundy.   It was a French
fief, which never had anything in common with

the German Empire. One of the first Capetians gave it to his brother in the eleventh century, and one of the first of the Valois gave it to his son in the fourteenth. By marriage, inheritance, and conquest, a considerable domain was rapidly formed, comprising the duchy of Burgundy, the counties of Flanders, Artois, Rethel, and Nevers, which were all fiefs of France; and Franche-Comté, the county of Namur, Brabant, Hainault, Zealand, Holland, Luxemburg, etc., which were lands of the Empire. Threatening Alsace, the duchy of Lorraine, and the confederated Swiss, this Burgundian state represented ancient Lotharingia accurately enough for Charles the Bold to make an attempt to restore the old Lotharingian kingdom.

Louis XI. succeeded in shattering this power, which had prevented France from making any progress toward the East, and which had even deprived her of lands already in her possession; for the limits of the Burgundian state in the north of France extended at one time to the Somme. France regained her territory by acquiring the duchy of Burgundy and the cities of the Somme.

Freed from the English, unfettered by the old feudal system, united and strong, it seemed as though France, at the close of the Middle Ages, would direct her attention to the North and East. For a time the dormant ambition to regain for the

French kingdom the old frontiers of Gaul awoke. But the French kings were seized with the mad desire—always to be deplored by France and Italy—to wage wars in Italy, wars which soon became European. Thus they let pass their great opportunity. The Swiss Confederation and Savoy each strengthened its power. The Netherlands were transferred by the daughter of Charles the Bold to the house of Austria, passing later on to Spain. Every enterprise of France against these countries was destined to provoke general wars.

All this territory without a master, between Germany and France, was a region of incoherence, accident, and chance. It was a soil suited to form peculiar kinds of governments, which have not had their parallel in the rest of Europe, such as the Swiss league ; or to produce agglomerations of territory, such as those of the Burgundian domain, which were not at all necessary in their origin, but which, by enduring, have modified history.

§ 20. *Formation of Spain.*

While France was being organized, two other new states, Spain and England, were undergoing this same process.

Ever since Spain had been conquered by the Saracens, she had been separated from Europe. In order to understand the indifference manifested by European nations toward this peninsula, when they were sending thousands of men to the Holy Land, it is necessary to bear in mind that no one in those days had any conception of a European community. This age, which was capable of finding precise rules of daily life, and of organizing a thousand petty governments around its towers, spires, and belfries, allowed itself to be guided by sentiments and ideas wholly outside the world of reality. The man of that period was wont to gaze at his feet, but when he lifted his head, his gaze was lost in the vast heavens.

We are inclined to say that the popes and kings would have done well to attack Islam in Europe rather than in Asia; but they never even thought of it. They were actuated by the feeling that there was no place more in need of deliverance, none whose deliverance would bring them more credit, than the spot where the Saviour had lived, and where he had lain buried for three days. They sent only a few isolated knights beyond the Pyrenees, and left to Spain the task of delivering herself.

The conflict lasted more than seven centuries. It was not conducted by one people against another, or by one ruler against another; several Christian kingdoms, which had been successively formed, fought with several small Arab states. In the fifteenth century the aspect of the Peninsula became less complex.   There were then only one Arab state, that of Granada, and four Christian kingdoms : Navarre, Portugal, Aragon, and Castile.   Navarre, which had been the most powerful kingdom, was now only a petty Pyrenean state.   Portugal, facing the Atlantic Ocean, sought her fortune in that direction.   Aragon, facing the Mediterranean, already coveted the peninsula and islands of Italy.   Castile, the heart of Spain, was the last combatant of the Mussulman, and finally conquered Granada.   Soon Castile, Aragon, Navarre, and Granada were united; and the new state constituted the great power of Spain, extending along both the Mediterranean and the ocean.

§ 21. *The Kingdom of England.*

Like the great peninsula of the Southwest, the islands of the Northwest remained a long time isolated from the rest of Europe.   The Continent sent them armed colonists, who were superimposed in layers more or less thick upon the old Celtic population.   The successive invaders were : Romans, whose last and least durable conquest was Britain; Anglo-Saxons and Scandinavians, who arrived in great numbers in a series of migrations; and, finally, Normans, that is to say, an army from French Normandy, which was transformed into a

permanent colony, and which in the course of
time was amalgamated with the rest of the population.

The conversion of the Anglo-Saxon kings to
Christianity again connected their island with
Christian Europe. Thus was born a Church of
England, daughter of the Church of Rome, and
she was at first respectful and obedient. The conquest of England by the Duke of Normandy, a
vassal of the King of France, also implicated the
insular realm in the history of France, and consequently in the affairs of the Continent. But
this external history had only a secondary importance for England.

The feudal wars of the English kings against
their suzerain, the King of France, and the Hundred Years' War itself, with its dramatic reverses
of fortune, count in the general history of England
only in so far as they influenced the constitutional
development of the kingdom.

The England of that time was a small country.
It did not embrace all the British Isles : for Wales,
though conquered, remained Wales ; Ireland, likewise conquered by the Norman kings, remained
Ireland ; and Scotland continued to be a separate
kingdom. In the Middle Ages England, properly
speaking, had the appearance of a great French
fief.

By the first Norman kings she was governed as

was no other country in the Middle Ages. The
Normans had accustomed themselves to habits of
discipline and order in the piratical expeditions
which they used to undertake, when they obeyed
sea-kings and shared their booty. These habits
they retained in Normandy, which, in consequence,
was the only French territory with a strong judiciary and internal peace. These habits they
also took with them to England. They divided
the country among themselves, just as their an-
cestors had formerly divided gold, silver, utensils,
cattle, and captives. They calculated the exact
value of their conquest by undertaking a methodical census of lands and men. Thus the Anglo-
Norman kings knew exactly what property and
power they possessed, things of which the German Emperor was wholly ignorant, and concerning which the King of France did not have much
knowledge.

They kept under discipline all their subjects,
whether noble or not, by retaining for themselves
and their officers superior judicial authority and
the direct services of all freemen. They had vassals who were very wealthy, but who did not possess principalities consisting of contiguous estates;
who were landlords, not seigneurs. The small extent of the country and its insular isolation were
favorable to the maintenance of good order by the
crown. In this fragment of island, between the

ocean and territories inhabited by a hostile race, like the Welsh and the Scots, an Englishman was English, and only English. There was no fluctuating frontier nor vague zone of territory. There was no great seigneur whose homage wavered between two masters hostile to each other, and who could call himself, as occasion demanded, French or German, like the Count of Flanders; French or Aragonese, like many a seigneur in the South; vassal of the King of France or of the Emperor, like the Count of Toulouse, Marquis of Provence.

This good order of a well-regulated monarchy and the power of the monarch produced an unexpected result, namely, political liberty. Just because the king had everything in his own hands, because the rights and duties of all were defined with precision, because each person easily came in contact with all, because people saw, knew, and elbowed each other, the resistance to a power that was too strong was easily organized, and with the first attempt attained its object. The Great Charter of John Lackland enacted that no freeman should be convicted in any way whatsoever, except by due judgment of his peers; and that no money impost should be levied without the common consent of the realm. These two articles gave England two great guarantees of liberty, the jury and Parliament.

English society did not break up into castes

separated from one another by habits and prejudices. It had grades, but not barriers. And at last the Saxons and Normans were amalgamated, and spoke a single national language. Thus England of the fifteenth century was more than a state; it was almost a nation.

The sea, over which she was afterward to rule, rendered her at this time no other service than to isolate her, to endow her with originality, and to inspire her with a national spirit, narrow, but lofty and proud. She had neither a great marine nor a great commerce. Her cities were quite small. She subsisted—very bountifully—on tillage and pasturage. She did not weave even the wool of her own sheep, but sold it to Flanders, which was her manufactory. She was likewise in close political relations with that country, which she already defended against the kings of France. Her vocation abroad was not yet revealed; but she had various powers in reserve: the power of a sanguine, vigorous, and vehement temperament, and the power which is produced by freedom and by the spirit of independence. These she was at first to waste in her civil and religious wars; but eventually she employed them to found an empire, the most extensive and flourishing that history has known.

§ 22. *General and Concluding Reflections on the Middle Ages.*

At the beginning of the ninth century Europe was divided into two very distinct historical regions. One was the Balkan Peninsula, where the old Empire still endured ; the other was complex, consisting of the Rhine region, where Carolingian energy had developed, and Rome, where the Papacy had preserved, but transformed, the tradition of a world power. At this time Gaul, Germany, and Italy were only dependencies of the Rhenish *Francia*, governed in temporal matters by the Emperor, in spiritual matters by the Pope. England under her Saxon and Danish kings, and Spain, which was in great part Moslem, had little or no importance in the Christian world.

Three great personages created the history of that time : the Pope, the Emperor of the West, and the Emperor of the East. The world had also three capitals : Rome, Aix-la-Chapelle, and Constantinople.

In the fifteenth century the Empire of the East disappears. The city of Constantine and the city of Pericles become Turkish. The Balkan Peninsula becomes an annex of Asia.

The Emperor of the West is now only a petty prince, occupied with the affairs of his house, powerless even in Germany, even in his hereditary countries. This *dominus mundi* is an object of derision. The Pope has emerged from the crisis of the Great Schism, weakened and imperilled. The Vicar of Christ has sunk to the rank of an Italian prince; he has a family to provide for, and, like the Emperor, his own petty private affairs to look after. Against his supremacy Wickliffe and Huss have spoken, and their words will not be lost.

The ecclesiastical and imperial past is crumbling in ruins on the countries with which it has been identified. The Rhine region has fallen into decay; Aix-la-Chapelle is only a memory. Germany and Italy, which restored the Empire in the tenth century, and on which the Empire subsisted, are now scarcely more than geographical expressions.

On the other hand, in the West and the East great innovations have been introduced. In the West, three organized entities, France, England, and Spain, are ready for modern life; in the East, outside the limits of the ancient Empire, within regions unknown to the ancients and regarded by them as abominable, have appeared Denmark, Sweden, Poland, Bohemia, Hungary, the Teutonic Knights, and the Sword-bearers.

In the last-mentioned countries an immense stretch of uncultivated territory has been reclaimed. It has its castles, palaces, cathedrals, and town-halls. It has its saints, kings, seigneurs, bishops, burgesses, artisans, and merchants. It has its men of learning. Good and solemn Latin is spoken in Bohemia, Poland, and Hungary. Prague has its university, modelled after that of Paris.

On the whole Continent and on the English island, an activity reigns, confused but singularly potent. There are more artisans, artists, statesmen, soldiers, and thinkers than ever existed in the ancient world. The intellect, although it has not found the true method of working, works more than ever before. It is a joy to anyone who loves life, to see it in such a state of effervescence.

From the tumultuous laboratory of the Middle Ages there is at length about to emerge an historical entity, greater and more potent than Greece and Rome, for these are magnified in our imaginations by prejudices of education. That entity is Europe.

CHAPTER IV.

MODERN TIMES.

§ 1. *General Characteristics.*

THE formation of states distinct from one another, each having its own character, passions, and interests, was destined to produce, as a necessary consequence, a conflict between these various elements. The coexistence of individuals, each of whom is his own master, and considers the absolute possession of himself the sovereign good, this juxtaposition without a hierarchy, these ambitions without a moderator, these pretensions without a common judge, were all causes of war.

It was certain that France would seek to extend her territory toward the north and east, now that she was protected on the two other sides by her natural frontiers; it was certain that France and Spain, now that each was unified, would quarrel in the Pyrenees, as neighbors often do; it was certain that the conflict between the Germans and the Turks, and between the Germans and the Slavs, would continue in the East; and certain that the competition between the maritime nations would not continue without the sound of cannon on all the seas—the North Sea, the Baltic, the Mediterranean, and the oceans. But, in addition to these causes, there were others that contributed to make war almost the normal condition of Europe in modern times.

The discovery of the New World and the establishment of active relations with Eastern Asia might have diminished the evils of European war, since they furnished states with an outlet for their energy. But the governments of Europe began by considering the colonies simply as countries to exploit. To reserve to themselves the benefits of exploitation they created monopolies, which they entrusted to armed companies. Since, on the other hand, political centralization had resulted in the transformation of commerce and industry—which formerly belonged to corporations —into state institutions, there were thenceforth national economic interests which became motives of war. The Europeans — Portuguese, Dutch, Spaniards, English, and French—did not content themselves with fighting in the two Indies to acquire territories and rights, nor with extending to Europe conflicts begun in the colonies; they even sought war on the Continent in order that they might extend it to the colonies.

The Reformation did not long remain an ecclesiastical affair; for as the State and the Church were closely connected, to reform the Church was a State affair. Where the Reformation succeeded it increased the authority of the sovereign, by giving him a fragment of the sole and universal authority of the Holy See. The king of a Protestant country was the supreme archbishop of that country, a localized Pope. Thus the first political effect of the Reformation (an effect that was afterward corrected) was to strengthen the monarchies by giving them new power, and to distinguish the European principalities more clearly from one another. Even if it had everywhere succeeded, it would have stimulated the rivalries between the states, for the very reason that it placed them in the hands of their respective rulers, and cut the sole bond by which they were still united. But the Reformation gained only partial victories over Catholicism.

It began by creating two parties in every country. Where these were approximately equal in power, they tried their strength in civil war. Moreover, there was formed an international Catholic party, and an international Protestant party; in France, Catholic Spaniards fought side by side with French Catholics against French, German, and English Protestants.

Thus the life of France, that of England, and still more that of Germany were profoundly troubled by

6

forays of religious hatred across the frontiers. Of course, politics did not blindly follow the guidance of religion. State policy silenced religious scruples. The Most Christian King of France who, as it was said, did not hesitate to bind the lilies to the crescent, made use of the Protestants against Austria; the three Catholic powers—Spain, France, and Austria—almost always treated each other as irreconcilable enemies. It is none the less true that the Reformation, on the one hand, and the Catholic reaction, on the other, were occasions of war, and that they embittered those wars which they did not cause.

The Renaissance was not simply an intellectual, any more than the Reformation was simply a religious, phenomenon. The Renaissance also strengthened the authority of the sovereign by restoring the cult of the ancient state, a state which was self-sufficing, and of which the *lex suprema* was self-advantage. The Renaissance, furthermore, diffused over Europe the political manners of Italy, where the principal states were wont to observe, to secretly watch, and to check one another, in order to maintain the equilibrium of their powers. As Italy was open to foreign nations, this scrutiny was also directed abroad. Italy was the birthplace of the ambassador, that pseudo-agent of concord and peace. Europe would certainly have learned political knavery without a master, but

she profited by the lessons which she received
from Italy. She fervently meditated the gospel
according to Machiavelli.

Thus the discovery of the New World, the Reformation, and the Renaissance made the modern
world pay its footing.

There was another more specific and direct
cause of war. Sovereignty was not a magistracy
or office, it was a piece of property. It was acquired by marriage or inheritance. Hence it happened that princes obtained possession of provinces
and even whole states, outside of their native land.
The house of Austria built up a remarkable empire, in which, by the side of its German domains,
it incorporated Burgundian, Slavic, and Hungarian
countries, Spain, and a great part of Italy. The
kings of France claimed succession to the duchy of
Milan and to the kingdom of Naples. Later, Louis
XIV. asserted his rights to the succession of Spain,
and exacted instalments of his inheritance before it
came into his possession. Thus natural groups, differing very much from one another, were embraced
in factitious monarchies. As there also remained
from the past the memory of a universal monarchy
—a phantom haunting the spirit of kings and statesmen—Charles V., Philip II., and Louis XIV. were accused of aspiring to form a " monarchy of Europe."

Royal marriages determined the future of the
Continent. If ever nuptials were bloody, it was

those of Maximilian of Austria with Mary of Burgundy, those of their son Philip with Joan of Spain, and those of Louis XIV. with Maria Theresa of Austria. In the wake of their bridal trains follow millions of shades of soldiers, killed on hundreds of battle-fields, and of other hapless victims of the evils of war.

War, which was almost perpetual, completed the work of political concentration in the different countries. Kings were obliged to secure considerable resources, which object they sought to attain by means of a better regulated administration. Hence, of necessity, their principal occupations were politics and war.

Every prince maintained a throng of political agents, some at home, others scattered in the courts of Europe. The sport of princes, in which "glory" was won, was to carry on successful intrigue and war. In diplomacy mercenary foreign agents were numerous, and foreign mercenaries abounded in the armies. In fact, throughout all Europe there existed a diplomatic and military "condottierism." The highest offices were sometimes attained by civil condottieri, of whom Mazarin and Alberoni are examples. Military condottieri became heroes in the eyes of monarchy, and were rewarded for their services; of these Prince Eugene of Savoy and Marshal Saxe are examples. Thus there was a political and also a mili-

tary profession; statesmen and soldiers led and disturbed the world.   The object of politics and war
was not merely to assure the existence or safety of
states; rulers intrigued because they had diplomats, and they made war because they had soldiers.
In these quarrels of kings the nations, as such, did
not actively participate; their part was only to suf-
fer the evils of war, to pay its costs, and to take
pride in the glory of their master when he won
victories.

Philosophers and savants strove to establish
principles and rules of justice above these conflicts, in order to prevent them or to diminish their
violence.   They framed the *droit des gens*, that is
to say, international law.   They condemned all
war which had not as motive the reparation of an
offence committed against law; they limited the
power of the conqueror over the conquered; and
they taught that treaties between states were inviolable, like contracts between individuals.   But
this code lacked an authority to suppress crimes
against the law of nations, a judge and an agency
to execute his decisions.   All these fine maxims,
without a single exception, were flagrantly violated
by the various governments, without a single exception.   Wars were waged without lawful reason;
the conquered were treated atrociously; agree-
ments were violated without scruple.

Only one general maxim regulated politics.   It

was understood among diplomats that it was the
interest of all that no state should become strong
enough to oppress the others.   This was the principle of the balance of power in Europe.   The
idea was excellent, but its application was peculiar.   If a state increased, and thus destroyed the
balance of power, its neighbors did not demand
that the newly acquired possessions should be re-
nounced : they sought compensation.   Poland was
a victim of this principle of compensation.   She
was torn to pieces, and the fragments were weighed
in a balance.   Maria Theresa found the act evil in
itself, but her chief complaint was that Prussia
and Russia had taken the best part.

There was, then, no counterpoise to all the
causes that had as common effect this state of
continual war.   A peace of several years' duration
was rare in these three centuries, and astonished
the world as an anomaly.   The kings boasted of
it, as if it were a sacrifice that they were making
for the "repose of their subjects."

It remains to show the results of all these conflicts—who gained thereby, and who lost.

§ 2. *Italy and Germany.*

That the modern era pressed heavily on Germany and Italy was the result of the logic of
events.   In the Middle Ages neither Italian polyarchy nor German anarchy was unseasonable ; but

they became anomalies after the establishment of centralized states, and these countries found by experience that it is not always well to be unlike one's neighbors.

They gave to the world the Renaissance and the Reformation, thus acquiring the glory of having exerted upon Europe a very strong intellectual, moral, and religious influence, and of having played a great part in the general history of civilization. This glory they owe, in part, to their genius, in part to the very causes of their political sufferings. The Renaissance had more energy and variety because Italy was vigorous and heterogeneous. The Reformation spread in Germany, because amid the disorders of this country it did not encounter an authority strong enough to check it, as in France, or to crush it, as in Spain; also because, of all Christian countries, Germany was the one in which the Church was guilty of the greatest abuses with the least concern as to the result.

Thus in both countries great evils produced certain striking compensations; but these, in turn, aggravated the evils. The Renaissance rendered the defects of the Italian system incurable; it was almost everywhere the servant of tyranny, whose egotism it developed. The Reformation added religious discord to German anarchy.

The decadence of Germany and Italy was very great. The expansion of Germany ceased. The

northeast of Europe was now colonized, and hence
had no more allurements for persons in quest of fortune and adventure. It was a period of adversity
for the Teutonic Order and the Hanse, which in
the preceding period had been the two great agen-
cies of emigration.

The knightly orders were impaired in their very
principle by the enfeeblement of the Christian
idea, of which they were a manifestation. The
Teutonic Knights who outlived the Crusades were
isolated in an age which no longer comprehended
the Crusades. They continued to wear the sign of
the Cross; but, as Luther once said, "What, for-
sooth, are crusaders who do not undertake crusades?" This question could not be answered.
But it is dangerous to cease to be useful. The
Teutonic Knights, having become useless, disappeared; a Hohenzollern, their last grand-master,
secularized the order, and became Duke of Prussia.

The Hanse, which was an international corpora-
tion, was seriously impaired by the formation of
the states of the North, each of which had its own
marine; and the discovery of the New World
completed this work of destruction. Henceforth
the Baltic was nothing compared with the great
oceans; the streets of Lubeck and Bremen became
silent. Moreover, Poland regained strength in
the sixteenth century; in the seventeenth, Sweden became a military state, and Russia appeared

on the scene. Germany again began her onward march in the eighteenth century; but it was Prussia that now made conquests on her own account, and she had to reckon with her Russian partner.

The expansion of Italy was also arrested. The Turks, Christopher Columbus, and Vasco de Gama killed Venice. The Adriatic declined in importance even more than the Baltic.

Italy and Germany, being thrown upon their own resources, were not capable of withstanding foreign attacks. Their weakness was a danger not merely to themselves but also to Europe. Notwithstanding all these wars, there was, after all, a kind of continental organism. It was bad for all Europe that parts of this organism were unhealthy, that they harbored and nourished the germ of war. The old region of the priesthood and of the Empire, exposed to the enterprises of modern statesmen, was too easily exploited. Italy and Germany had neither a head nor a heart to resent the injuries which they thus received from all quarters. In fact, they were by their own profession battle-fields of Europe.

§ 3. *The Italian Field of Battle—The King of Sardinia.*

"Italy will act for herself" (*Italia fara da se*), exclaim the Italian patriots of to-day. The potentates of modern Europe used to say, "What action shall we take in Italy?" Spain, France, and Austria played chess there during three centuries.

In the fifteenth and sixteenth centuries the kings of France claimed to be the successors of the Visconti of Milan and the Angevins of Naples; but there had been Aragonese at Naples, and the Empire had rights over Milan. Thus Spain and Austria played against France, and won the game. In the seventeenth century Hapsburgs of Spain and Austria, and Bourbons of France sought every occasion for conflict with each other; they met on the soil and seas of Italy. Then came the preparations for the Spanish succession, and the succession itself. Who was to secure possession of Milan and Naples? The fate of war—and it was a dreadful war—decided in favor of Austria in 1715. During the remainder of the eighteenth century Italy was at the disposal of Europe. She was the country where principalities were found for throneless princes. Here Elizabeth Farnese, wife of the Bourbon Philip V. of Spain, provided her sons with a kingdom and a duchy. After the war of the Polish succession Stanislas Leczinski, father-in-law of Louis XV., being without an asylum, France provided him with the duchy of Lorraine; and Francis, Duke of Lorraine, son-in-law of the Emperor, became ruler of Tuscany. The courtesy shown to the father-in-law of Louis

XV. was also extended to the son-in-law of Charles
VI. The *membra mortua* of this *caput mortuum*
were distributed to every comer. In twenty-one
years Sicily changed masters four times; Parma,
three times in seventeen years.

Such misery and indignity seemed to be the final
destiny of Italy. Nevertheless, an innovation,
which in the issue became of great importance,
appeared in the northwest of the Peninsula. In
the perpetual conflicts between the Hapsburgs and
the Bourbons, the state of the dukes of Savoy,
situated on two opposite sides of the Alps, played
the double rôle imposed upon it by its geographical situation. There was no prince who could be
less trusted than the Duke of Savoy, "the door-
keeper of the Alps." Several times Savoy was
wrested from him by France, and he had to cede
to Henry IV. Bresse, Bugey, Valromey, and the
country of Gex. On the other hand, Geneva
maintained her independence against him, and the
Swiss Confederation became more consolidated.
Then the house of Savoy sought its fortune in
Italy.

To Piedmont it added the duchy of Montferrat
and a part of the Milanese territory. In every
great European treaty the duke gained something
by exacting payment for his alliances, in the trans-
ference of which from one camp to another he
excelled. While he was occupied in eating the

first scales of the " Italian artichoke," he displayed a remarkable appetite for such a mediocre prince. This was manifested by the fact that he claimed his share of the Spanish and Austrian successions. The War of the Spanish Succession gave him Sicily, which he soon exchanged for Sardinia; but he retained the title of king which he had borne during his short possession of Sicily. Thus he entered the fraternity of sovereigns; he was King of Sardinia and even King of Jerusalem. He wore clothes too long and too large for a person of his size, but he was destined to grow until they fitted him. The only ruler in Italy who shared with him the honor of having a royal title was the King of Naples. But Italy proper was in the north. Here was the field of battle between France and Austria; here laurels were to be gathered, provinces to be won; here was Monza, the sanctuary where the Iron Crown awaited a royal head.

§ 4. *The German Field of Battle—Prussia and Austria.*

It was in Germany that the great conflicts between the Bourbons and the Hapsburgs occurred. French politics played a winning game in the disorganized body of the Empire. France subsidized the Electors, and at times was in hopes of purchas-

ing the imperial crown.   She subsidized the Protestant princes, the natural enemies of Catholic
Austria.   She subsidized the Catholic princes,
who as princes were enemies of the imperial
power.   She knew the exact value of a prince of
a given rank, of a minister, counsellor, or mistress;
Versailles, in fact, had a regular tariff of German
consciences.

In the seventeenth century the armies of Europe
overran the region between the Rhine and the Vistula, the Alps and the seas of the North.   Here,
during the Thirty Years' War, French armies
went to settle the old quarrel between the Bourbons and the Hapsburgs, and to ruin the latter's
pretensions to the sovereignty of Europe.   Here
Spanish armies upheld the cause of Catholic
orthodoxy.   Here Danish and Swedish armies defended the Protestant cause, and, at the same
time, continued the combat for the Baltic, begun
in the Middle Ages.   In fact, all these pious Catholics and Protestants were greedy and grasping.
Finally, Germany, which was divided between the
two parties, complicated the horrors of foreign war
by engaging in civil war.   The evils that this country suffered cannot be described.   Here, during
thirty years, war maintained war.   Friends and
enemies subsisted on the soil and its inhabitants,
feasting after days of famine, making up for their
abstinence by debauchery, for their hunger by or-

gies, returning evil for evil. All this they did by force of habit, and because in great crises man returns very quickly to his original instincts, those of a vicious animal. Germany was covered with ruined villages and towns. In more than one province, where everything except the trees had been levelled to the ground, briers, wild beasts, and cannibals made their appearance.

When the diplomats of Europe, after five years of ceremony, framed the Peace of Westphalia, it was found that Germany was officially left open to the foreigner. The King of Sweden, as a German prince, entered the Diet, in which the King of Denmark already had a seat. The King of France became a member of the Rhenish League, which had been organized by him. The sovereignty of the princes and cities of the Empire was recognized, and the imperial authority was annihilated. The high contracting powers had the right to maintain this anarchy, for they were the guarantors of the Peace of Westphalia. Hence Germany had no long breathing-time after this terrible war. Bourbons and Hapsburgs met there in the seventeenth and eighteenth centuries whenever a war broke out in Europe. England also went there to conquer America and India.

Whence was the remedy to come? For in Germany, as in Italy, the misery and indignity were too much to bear. Either of the two states

of the Eastern frontier was capable of assuming
the hegemony; accordingly they contended for its
possession, and their rivalry aggravated the disorders of Germany.   Moreover, in the eighteenth
century, Prussia and Austria were European rather
than German powers.

We shall soon encounter them again.   In the
period of the Middle Ages, starting with Germany, we turned our attention to the East; afterward we passed to the West, and dwelt upon its
history, because the West gave birth to France,
Spain, and England, and formed the principal theatre of European history.   In the modern period,
the most important events happened in the East.
Hence it is now necessary to follow a different order and begin with the West.

§ 5. *The Intermediate Region.*

In the intermediate region France gained ground.
In the South, during the reign of Henry IV., her
territory was increased by the addition of various
small districts, wrested from the Duke of Savoy.
In the centre and North she exacted the price
of her victories over both branches of the Hapsburgs.

Here she had to contend, in the sixteenth century, with Charles V., who acted in a two-fold
capacity.   As Emperor, he defended the rights

of the Empire in Alsace and Lorraine; as heir of the Burgundian dukes, he was owner of the Netherlands and Franche-Comté, and also claimed Burgundy, which Louis XI. had seized. Charles V. did not succeed in securing possession of Burgundy, notwithstanding his persistent efforts, for he was as infatuated a Burgundian as his rival, Francis I., was a persistent Visconti. The minds of these first heroes of modern politics were occupied with the ideas and habits of the preceding age.

When Charles V. abdicated, the Burgundian provinces, the Netherlands, and Franche-Comté passed to Philip II., King of Spain, while Ferdinand, the brother of Charles, succeeded to the imperial throne, and thus continued the series of Hapsburg emperors. The history of the acquisitions of France in the intermediate region mingles, thenceforward, with the history of her long warfare against the Spanish and German branches of the Hapsburgs.

From Spain Louis XIV. took Franche-Comté; but he succeeded in detaching from the Netherlands only Artois and certain cities of Flanders. From the Empire France won at first the three bishoprics, Metz, Toul, and Verdun; then Alsace without Strasburg; and then Strasburg. It was not by pure violence that France made these acquisitions. Metz, Toul, and Verdun were annexed

with the consent of German princes, whom Henry
II. had assisted in their revolts against Charles V.;
and Alsace was acquired by Richelieu with the
army which had, so to speak, made itself proprietor of this country. It would be disingenuous to
vindicate all the political measures of France; but
one can justly assert that the French of the seventeenth century, in taking Alsace, did not tear men
from a fatherland. At that time there was no
French fatherland in the present sense of the
word; still less was there a German fatherland.
The politics and armies of France did not cut into
the living flesh.

The acquisition of the three bishoprics and Alsace rendered inevitable that of Lorraine. This
French country was often occupied, during the
wars between the Bourbons and the Hapsburgs,
by the armies of France before becoming a French
province.

§ 6. *Provinces Remaining under Hapsburg Rule.*

Franche-Comté, Alsace, Lorraine, Artois, and
French Flanders were the districts acquired by
France in the intermediate region during the
modern period; the remainder of this region escaped her grasp. But Spain did not retain the
Netherlands; and the latter did not remain united.
In spite of geographical contiguity, there were

7

great differences between the seventeen provinces.
Some were maritime, others continental; some
were rich, others poor; some were municipal, others feudal; and some were German, others Wal-
loon. In each of them, and in each of the fragments of which they were composed, in the various
fiefs, communes, and corporations, life was too intense for all these individual beings to long endure
the system of the Spanish monarchy.

They endured it during the lifetime of Charles
V. The vaster and more heterogeneous the monarchy became, the less was the oppression of an
absolute ruler to be feared. Moreover, Charles
V. had the rare merit of reflecting in his person
the diversity of his Empire. He spoke all the
languages of his subjects, and knew how to com-
port himself, according to the occasion, as emperor,
king, count, nobleman, or burgher. But when he
detached the Netherlands from the Empire to give
them to Spain, the dire consequences of matrimonial politics appeared.

The marriage of Maximilian of Austria with
the daughter of the Burgundian, Charles the Bold,
was comprehensible; the states of Burgundy
bordered on the Empire, and were, in large part,
even countries of the Empire. Charles V., pos-
sessor of the Netherlands by right of inheritance,
was also sovereign by virtue of his title of Emperor.
But when, through the sole right of ownership,

the Netherlands were given to a Spanish and Italian king, violence was done to the natural order of things, and produced a revolt.

§ 7. *Separation of the Netherlands.*

The political resistance offered by the Netherlands to the despotism of Philip II., who violated their ancient privileges, was strengthened by religious passions. The Northern provinces had adopted Protestantism with fervor and with a sort of sombre enthusiasm; whereas their sovereign was the enthusiastic and sombre champion of Catholicism. During the conflict with Spain these provinces united. They tried at first to conform to European traditions by placing a prince at their head; afterward they were content to be merely, "Their High Mightinesses the States General of the United Provinces." As to the provinces of the South, after many revolts they remained subjected to the King of Spain. At the close of the sixteenth century the separation of the North and the South was accomplished.

Thenceforth the future Holland and Belgium followed their separate destinies. The latter, curtailed on the south by France, was severed from the Spanish monarchy and given to Austria by the treaties that regulated the Spanish succession. Thus it passed from the elder branch of the Hapsburgs to the younger, which still possessed it at the outbreak of the French Revolution.

§ 8. *The United Provinces.*

The United Provinces became a European power. They had colonies, an admirable marine, a great commerce, prosperous industries, and hence money, which, especially in the seventeenth century, formed the sinews of politics and war. Their politics were conducted by men who employed all the finesse of diplomacy in the difficult government of a federation of provinces, each of which had its own privileges, and was itself only an aggregate of privileged entities. This danger, to which a little, rich, republican state was exposed in the midst of arrogant and famished monarchies, kept its political spirit constantly awake. For purposes of war they had an aristocratic military force, the heads of which belonged to the house of Orange. In time of danger, when it was necessary to arouse and unite the national forces, the princes of Orange, who were related to the royal families of Europe, were able temporarily to transform the republic into a monarchy under the form of the stadtholdership.

For all these reasons, and because the republic was young, because it had the vitality of the many political bodies which it allowed to subsist within itself, because its energy was sustained by passions which were at once provincial, feudal, municipal, and corporative, as well as political and religious, the United Provinces wrested from the King of Spain the recognition of their independence. They defended it against Louis XIV., formed a strong coalition against France, aided their stadtholder, William of Orange, to ascend the throne of England, and finally humiliated the great King of France. This was the heroic period of their history. Such efforts, however, could not long be sustained.

If, by an extraordinary combination of circumstances, a state occupies a position in the world disproportional to its real powers, it will be brought back to the limits which it has overstepped. Holland, which in the seventeenth century was a powerful ship of war, was in the eighteenth century only a " sloop which England had in tow."

§ 9. *The Swiss Cantons.*

During this same period another republican state, the league of the Swiss cantons, developed in the intermediate region. But this remarkable body could not, like the United Provinces, adopt a European policy. It had neither seaboard, nor a great commerce, nor great industries, nor much money. While Switzerland, which was formed of fragments of nations, awaited the time when she was to become neutral among the nations, she sold her soldiers to any one who paid for them. The King of France finally obtained the preference in this trade. The Swiss were to be the last defenders of the flag of the *fleur-de-lis* in August, 1792, and in July, 1830.

The United Provinces and the Swiss Confederation both secured the recognition of their independence in 1648, the former by a separate treaty with Spain, the latter by the terms of the Treaty of Westphalia. Thus both derived great profit from the victories of France over the Hapsburgs. Moreover, France had aided the United Provinces in their revolt against Spain. This was not, indeed, due to disinterested motives on the part of France. When her kings made themselves the protectors of the small and the weak, they were not actuated by chivalric sentiment. Nevertheless, it is an honor to France that her victories indirectly resulted in giving to the political world two new and free states.

§ 10. *France.*

In modern times France followed the impulse which had already been given to her destiny in the Middle Ages. The French kings completed

the formation of the national territory by acquiring Brittany through marriage, Rousillon by conquest, Bearn and Navarre on the accession of
Henry IV.   We have followed their progress in
the intermediate region.   The acquisition of Corsica, made at the same time as that of Lorraine,
completed France as she was constituted before
1789.

Within this monarchy the provincial differences
were gradually effaced, though they never wholly
disappeared. The old privileges of the various countries, where they had not been abolished, became a
dead letter; likewise those of the manors and communes.   But these empty structures—provinces,
municipalities, and feudal lordships — cumbered
France, and incommoded her life. The power that
turned them into ruins would not, or could not,
remove the débris, which caused much disorder in
the constitution of France.   The resistance of such
vestiges of the past was encountered by the great
ministers of France, by those of the time of her full
glory, and by those of the close of the ancient régime, for example, Colbert and Turgot.   The old
monarchy shone in Europe with great brilliancy.
It contributed to the sum total of the greatness of
France the majesty of Louis XIV., which was
a real majesty.   But the monarchy did not establish a system of government and administration
adapted to a unified country.   It did not provide

itself with a good financial and military system; it did not give the country a good judicial and economic system. To speak the truth in all its nakedness, French kings knew how to exact obedience, but they did not know how to govern.

In their foreign policy they met with considerable success, and they also made great mistakes. The conflict with the house of Austria was at first imposed upon them. In attempting to break the circle enclosing France, Francis I., Henry II., Henry IV., Richelieu, and Mazarin maintained a proper and legitimate line of policy and warfare; and it was their good fortune to save the independence of Europe, while thus working for the greatness of France. But the monarchy, victorious in the middle of the seventeenth century, soon abused its victory. The claim to the Spanish succession, which at the present day is regarded as a chimera, was in accordance with the spirit of former politics; but it required a prudence and an attitude of conciliation that were wanting. Foreign nations, one after another, or all simultaneously, became imbued with hatred against France. Europe, thus united against the French by the French themselves, watched every measure and every intention of the King of France. The progress, slow but constant, which he had made during a century along the frontiers of the North and East, was arrested. France ceased to be the directing power which grouped around her the most diverse forces, guided events, and, when necessary, brought them into existence. The seventeenth century belonged to the Bourbons in combat with the Hapsburgs; the eighteenth century belonged to new powers.

It is always to be regretted that the foreign policy of France was absorbed in the affairs of the Continent, to the neglect of the rest of the world, whose history had become implicated in that of Europe. France, an oceanic and a Mediterranean power, was destined to play a very important rôle in Africa, Asia, and America. She had undertaken crusades; she early had bold explorers; she possessed Marseilles, Bordeaux, Nantes, and Havre; and she had excellent seafaring populations—the Normans, Bretons, Basques, and Provençals. She is calumniated when accused of being incapable of colonization. Her colonial history is a glorious one. She made an excellent beginning in the formation of a French empire beyond seas. Francis I., Henry IV., Richelieu, and Colbert saw what France could and should do; but continental politics absorbed all her strength and thought.

To humble the house of Austria was at first a necessity; and this afterward became a watchword mechanically handed down from king to king. The great successes of the French diplomats and generals in the sixteenth and seventeenth centuries aroused the emulation of their successors, even when Austria was no longer an enemy. The habit had been formed of waging war in the Netherlands, in Germany, and in Italy. It seemed as though glory could not be acquired on other fields of battle. The desire was to win it on this classic theatre of war, whence the tidings of victory would be brought to Versailles by a courier galloping at full speed. To this must be added the circumstance that in France the third estate counted for almost nothing in the body politic; the merchants could not make their voices heard, as in England.

The French nobility had ceased to be a feudal body, and had become a brilliant military society; but it had never become accustomed to marine service. Its chiefs served only in the army. "The admiral," when there was one, was usually a courtier, who was not even a fresh-water sailor. Indeed, Versailles, where monarchy slept, was not even washed by a river. The labors of Hercules were necessary to furnish it with drinking-water.

§ 11. *Spain.*

The formation of the Spanish state was completed at the beginning of modern times, a single absolute monarchy being substituted for the old feudal monarchies. Thereupon Spain, emerging from the lists in which she had so long fought the infidel, suddenly conquered the richest parts of the New World. She was at the same time entangled in all the affairs of the Continent by the family alliance concluded between Castile and Austria.

To people and organize her colonies, to conduct a line of policy which involved her in conflicts with other European states, to protect her possessions in Italy, Franche - Comté, and Flanders, all the powers of Spain, even if nourished and increased, would not have sufficed. Her government ruined her by the exercise of a sombre, solemn, and stupid despotism, and by the infatuation of a religious fanaticism that offered up to God an *auto-da-fe* not merely of thousands of individuals, but also of the commerce, industry, and activity of Spain.

During the Middle Ages the Orientals had produced in this country marvels of labor; but modern Spain was invaded by an Oriental somnolence, which ended in lethargy. This kingdom, the valiant adversary of France in the sixteenth and the beginning of the seventeenth century, was forced to pay the expenses of all the French wars, and France supported all the revolts against Spain. In 1700, when the Spanish branch of the Hapsburgs was withered, Louis XIV. gave to Spain an off-shoot of his dynasty. To fix it in the soil, twelve years of war were necessary, at the end of which period the ruin of Spain was completed.

When Europe settled the Spanish succession, she rendered Spain a service by relieving her of her Belgian and Italian dependencies. A policy of repose and repair would have restored Spain, rich in the gifts of nature; but the new king from Versailles was a sort of lazy monk, tormented by dreams of love and ambition. Moreover, the habit of mingling in European politics was established at the Escurial. Herein also tradition asserted its sway over the mind, and led it astray. Spain had not time to restore her strength. At first adventurers and then ministers of state attempted to rejuvenate her. They desired to diminish the number of court parasites, who devoured what little substance remained; to drive the plunderers from the administration; to reform taxation; to pay the judges; to clothe, arm, and feed the soldiers; to build arsenals; to place ships in the ports, cannon on the ramparts, workmen in the factories, and husbandmen in the fields. The boldest of them also undertook to recover the Spanish intellect from the sway of the Church. They met with successes, but of a moderate and transient nature; they galvanized the body politic, which then relapsed into lifelessness.

England made a breach in the colonial empire of Spain, a remarkable empire, which the mother-country did not colonize, which she desired only to exploit, and which she did not know how to exploit. Into these colonies she introduced all the vices of her political, social, and religious life, her despotism which carefully hindered all expansion of commerce and industry, her idle and arrogant nobles, her ignorant officials, her monks, and her lethargy.

§ 12. *England.*

The history of England was exactly the reverse of that of Spain. The constitution established in England was that of a free country. She went through crises of extreme violence, such as the Wars of the Roses, the religious revolutions of the sixteenth century, and the religious and political revolutions of the seventeenth century. Sects and parties abounded in the land. On the Continent a little country thus troubled would have paid for such violent disorders with the loss of life and independence. But the sea performed its functions, and protected the island which was to rule over it.

Three passions animated England: loyalty, hatred of popery, and attachment to certain principles of political liberty. The first two were the most active; they determined England's history and explain its contradictions. Loyalty, on several occasions, made Englishmen support a despotism such as was unknown in monarchical France.

Thus it protected Charles I. for a long time; re-
called Charles II. from exile; permitted this king
and his brother to commit the greatest offences;
sulked with George III., and disturbed the security of the house of Hanover. Hatred of popery
raised up Cromwell, killed Charles I., and exiled
James II.

From the conflict between these two chief passions England's liberty finally emerged. The nation, even when it allowed the kings to do as
they pleased, retained a faithful recollection of the
charter of John Lackland. It was always perilous for the king, except in great emergencies, to
deprive an Englishman of trial by jury; and
it was still more perilous for him to raise a tax
without the consent of Parliament. Thus, when
the quarrel between the loyalists and the anti-
papists had been settled, and foreigners, first a
Dutchman and then the Hanoverians, succeeded
to the throne of England, the dominant passion
became that of liberty.

Then England began to govern herself. Parliament furnished the king with a ministry, which
could do almost everything without the king,
but which could do nothing without Parliament.
Against its own government the country defended
itself by means of its rights and liberties. It had
private rights, whereby the person of an Englishman, his domicile, and his purse were rendered

inviolable against all illegal acts; and public
rights, namely, the right of complaint and petition,
the right of meeting, the right of association, the
right to speak and to write. But this magnificence
concealed certain weaknesses and deformities: an
irrational electoral system, scandalous corruption
of the voter by the candidate and of the member
elect by the ministry; and the persistence of religious intolerance and of strange vestiges of the
past. No matter! England was free; indeed, in
the eighteenth century she was the only free nation in the world.

After the death of Elizabeth, Scotland and England had the same king. Ireland had been reduced to the condition of an ever-suppurating
wound; of all English deformities this was the
ugliest. But the personal union with Scotland,
which prepared the way for the fusion of the two
countries, delivered England from the neighbor-
hood of a possible enemy, and assured her freedom of action abroad.

Her national policy—interrupted and disturbed
in the sixteenth and seventeenth centuries by internal revolutions—was directed by various motives: by the proud remembrance, preserved on
the royal escutcheon, of the time when an English
king ruled over France; by the ambition to pa-
rade on the Continent ("The one whom I protect
is master," said Henry VIII.); by the feeling

against the Catholicism personified in Philip II.; and by commercial interests. The Stuarts sold the foreign policy of the crown to Louis XIV., in order to employ its market price against the public liberties and religious convictions of their subjects. But as soon as England was her own mistress, she cast aside all prejudices, fantasies, and weaknesses. She followed without scruple a practical line of policy. She mingled in the affairs of the Continent, where she played an important rôle, without self-sacrifice, since she incurred no danger, and did not employ her vital forces. She worked for the maintenance of the balance of power, her efforts always being directed against France, to prevent the latter from extending her sway over the Netherlands, and from dominating over Spain. And she always created or seized opportunities to increase her colonial empire.

In fact, her vocation had been revealed to her; the sea had at length seduced England. She was the last of the colonizing powers to set to work; but it was fortunate for her that others had taken possession of the countries of gold and spices. Her first colonists established themselves on the coasts of North America—on stubborn soil. She had no occasion to deprive them of the products of their labor; and she allowed them to work in their own way. Among these colonists were many who went beyond sea to seek, not profit nor adventure, but freedom to worship God according to their conscience. Gradually the elements of a people were gathered there. It is true that this people finally claimed the right of independence; but it is no small honor to have entirely created a nation like the United States. England found, moreover, some consolation in her greatly increased commerce with these Anglo-Saxon lands after they secured their independence.

Besides, she retained Canada, which she had conquered from France. She took possession of islands, and secured well-situated stations, in all the seas. She wrested from France the empire of India. In short, at the outbreak of the French Revolution, with her navy, her merchant marine, her immense commerce, and her awakening manufacturing activity, she was the great maritime nation of Europe. Protected from the convulsions of the Continent by her isolation, her solid constitution, and her customs, she was destined to be the most formidable enemy of France.

§ 13. *The East—Prussia.*

Let us now return to the North and East, where events of the greatest importance had happened. Among the old powers some had decayed; others, like Austria and Prussia, had prospered. Russia, a new power of considerable importance, had appeared on the scene.

The Hohenzollerns had completed the formation of Prussia. As Electors of Brandenburg they had, early in the seventeenth century, inherited Rhenish duchies and the Prussia of the Teutonic Knights, now transformed into a duchy. Thenceforth a single prince ruled on the Vistula, the Elbe, and the Rhine. Nothing was less necessary or less natural; for these three countries scarcely knew one another, had no common traditions, and did not resemble one another. But all three were harassed by war in the seventeenth century. The Rhenish duchies formed a field of battle for France and Holland against Austria and Spain; Brandenburg served the same purpose for Sweden against Austria; and in Prussia there were conflicts between Poles, Swedes, Austrians, and Russians. The necessity of being ready for all conflicts, since the Hohenzollerns were sure to be implicated in them, imposed upon these princes constant effort, a constant combat for existence.

To fuse into one state provinces whose history and customs were so different, to employ their powers for common ends, to unite the links of the broken chain, was the plan which was enjoined by circumstances, and which was executed. Magdeburg, Halberstadt, and Minden, which were acquired in 1648, were successive steps on the route from Berlin to the Rhine. Pomerania, acquired in two instalments, gave Brandenburg a seaboard. After the conquest of Silesia the realm was flanked by mountains. After the spoliation of Poland, Brandenburg and Prussia, the two essential parts of the state, were amalgamated.

After these annexations the state of the Hohenzollerns remained a singular edifice, consisting of a body and two wings, one of which stretched out, broken in fragments, to the Rhine, and the other to the Niemen; but the government held together this scattered power. Rulers whose territories were fields of battle were necessarily military autocrats, who exacted passive obedience from their subjects. *Nicht raisonniren,* " No reasoning here," was their motto. It was also very necessary for them to be frugal and to turn to account all their productive powers. And in this Germany, in which the smallest potentates took pride in disfiguring the splendors and in parodying the vices of Versailles, patriots looked with pride upon princes who were always toiling, and who boasted that they were the first servants of their state.

Moreover, the Hohenzollerns were distinguished among German rulers by a superior dignity. The Teutonic Order, after its defeat in the fifteenth century, had been obliged to become the vassal of the King of Poland. Thus the Duke of Prussia, the successor of the Order, did homage to a foreigner. But the Electors of Brandenburg, after inheriting the duchy, desired to free themselves from this humiliating obligation. A war having broken out between the kings of Sweden and Poland soon after the Peace of Westphalia, the Elector-Duke allowed his allegiance to vacillate from the one to the other, that is to say, he betrayed the one after the other, in order to secure from both the recognition of his sovereignty. At the end of the war he was, in fact, a sovereign. There was a corner of the earth where the Hohenzollern had above him no one except God.

In the Germany of that time, however, there could be no king, because the Emperor was, in theory, the sole sovereign; but a German prince could be king of a foreign country. The Elector of Saxony was King of Poland; the Elector of Brandenburg had the ambition to be King of Prussia, and he was crowned in 1700, with the assent of the Emperor. A few years later a Hanoverian inherited the throne of England. Prussia was insignificant compared with England, or even with Poland. The rulers of these two countries regarded themselves as exalted potentates by the side of their brother of Prussia, but they were not masters in their own kingdoms, and their quality of foreign king almost effaced that of prince of the Empire. Prussia, though considered a foreign land, was German; the royal power was absolute; the kingdom, just because it was small and modest, did not absorb the Hohenzollerns. They became European princes, but remained princes of Germany, and the royal dignity gave them greater authority in the Empire. For these reasons they were in a less brilliant but more favorable position than the Electors of Hanover and Saxony.

Brandenburg had for a long time been marked out as the enemy of Austria, and had, since the sixteenth century, inspired the latter with a feeling of inquietude. Their inequality was great, but Brandenburg represented the opposition of North Germany against Southern Germany, of Protestantism against Catholicism. When the elector was made king, a conflict between the two houses became inevitable. Moreover, Prussia found compensation for her greater feebleness in the superiority of her government. The second King of Prussia, Frederick William I., was still very insignificant and humble compared with the Emperor. But he ruled over 2,500,000 subjects; he had an army almost equal in number to that of Austria, and consisting of better material; his finances were in very good order, he had no debts, and savings had accumulated in the treasury.

To all these resources Frederick II., King of Prussia, added genius. He had an intellect and a will that wielded power. He professed the greatest contempt for custom, traditions, and rights; and defeated the Emperor more frequently and more completely than was proper for a member of the Empire; he, a new-comer, vanquished old monarchies. He not only increased his territory by annexing Silesia and Polish provinces, but also created modern Prussia, and forced an entrance into the fraternity of the great powers. His work had the character, the promptitude, and the importance of a revolution. His state, which he advanced to the first rank, did not resemble any other. It was German without being German. It was an upstart, and yet it had ancient traditions. The Hohenzollerns were old like the Empire; Brandenburg had been an electorate since the thirteenth century; and Prussia was the heroic domain of the mediæval German knights. This state was at once old and young. It had the choice between two destinies, for it was adapted to the work of reaction or to the work of revolution. It was a formidable two-edged weapon, which struck with the one edge or the other according to time and place.

§ 14. *Austria.*

When we left Austria, the domain of the Hapsburg house consisted of Austria, Styria, Tyrol, Carinthia, and Trieste. Partly German, partly

Slavic, partly Italian, these lands formed the foundation of the future tower of Babel, at the base of
which a confusion of tongues was to burst forth
in our day.

Four causes determined the modern destiny of
the Hapsburgs: the marriages which made Charles
V. heir of the house of Burgundy and of the
Spanish crown; the loyalty of Austria to Catholicism; the custom that became established in
Germany of always giving the Empire to Austria;
and, finally, the acquisition of Bohemia and Hungary in the sixteenth century, and of a portion of
Poland in the eighteenth.

It was the union of the Austrian, Burgundian,
and Spanish inheritances that brought the Hapsburgs and the Bourbons into conflict. It was because Austria was the champion of Catholicism
that France found allies in Germany, and, waging
war there, was able to aid the German princes to
become petty sovereigns. The imperial office gave
some cohesion to the incongruous aggregate of the
monarchy. Finally, the acquisition of Bohemia,
Hungary, and a part of Poland made Austria a
state that marked a transition between Western
and Eastern Europe.

§ 15. *Essential Difference between Prussia and Austria.*

By acquiring the Hungarian kingdom, a Slavic kingdom, and the fragment of another Slavic country, the head of the house of Hapsburg seemed to be performing the functions of the old march of Austria, erected in the Middle Ages to defend the frontiers of Christianity against the Slavs of the Danube and against the Avars. His prosperity had been more brilliant than that of the King of Prussia, successor of those margraves of the North whose early function was to oppose the Slavs of the Elbe; but his prosperity was also less substantial.

The King of Prussia ruled over several countries that were not German in origin—Brandenburgh, Lusatia, Silesia, Pomerania, Prussia, and Poland; but, excepting Poland, all had become German. The last of the old Prussians were dead; a few words of their language survived, an object of curiosity to philologists. Dead also were the Slavs of Brandenburg and Pomerania. Slavs survived in Lusatia and Silesia, but submerged in the German population, an object of curiosity to ethnographers. The King of Prussia, Elector of Brandenburg, had taken for his electoral title the name of *Brannybor*, a Slavic town, and for his royal title the name of Prussia, a Lithuanian country; but these foreign names were like rich spoils —*spolia opima*—worn by a German king in memory of the victory of his race over hostile races.

In the Austrian monarchy, on the other hand, there was a Bohemia entirely inhabited by Tsechs, a Hungary entirely inhabited by Hungarians, and a Transylvania entirely inhabited by Roumanians. The Slavs were alive in all Illyria; the Italians, in the Italian dependencies; and the Poles, in Poland. When, later on, the national spirit, at the time of its awakening, rebelled against the compacts which had included in one body so many diverse entities, Austria found herself seriously menaced. But in the period with which we are now dealing, this danger was not yet perceptible, for the Hapsburgs ruled tranquilly in the eighteenth century. The monarchy suffered from a certain sluggishness; it was clumsy and not well in hand, but it obeyed.

Only two facts remain to be noted. Austria allowed Frederick II., King of Prussia, to secure possession of Silesia, and this monarch organized a coalition of German princes against Austria, when she undertook to claim Bavaria; in fact, he forbade all increase of Austrian territory in Germany. On the other hand, the head of the Austrian house, having become King of Hungary, regarded it as his mission to drive back the infidels, and to recover from them the Hungarian territory, the greater part of which was in possession of the Turks. Austria did, in fact, recover it, and the empire of the Hapsburgs thus became a great Danubian power. Note the omens: a route closed toward the North and West, and opened toward the East.

§ 16. *Mediæval Russia.*

While the two German states of the East were thus advancing on Slavic soil, a new Eastern state was completing its formation, a great Slavic power was being organized.

Thus far we have been able to neglect Russia. She had almost nothing in common with Europe, which terminated with the frontiers of Germany and her dependencies. During the whole of the Middle Ages Russian history is lost in the confused annals of Eastern Europe. In the ninth century Russia was separated from the Baltic by tribes of the Finnish and Lithuanian race. Between her and Carolingian Germany were the Slavs of the Elbe, of the Oder, of Bohemia, of Moravia, of Lusatia, and of Poland. Her intercourse with the Euxine and the Danube was intercepted by Asiatic tribes, which successively occupied these regions.

Thus ramparts of tribes stood between the Russians and the Elbe and Danube, which were then the frontiers of history; also between the Russians and the Baltic and Euxine, those two gulfs of the two great historic seas. It was necessary to pierce these masses in order to reach Europe.

It was Europe that first advanced toward Russia. At the close of the ninth century adventurers coming from Sweden established their sway over the Slavs of Novgorod. They quickly forgot their Scandinavian origin. Thus the first Russian country, of which Novgorod, and then Kief, were the principal cities, appeared on the map of the great plain of the Northeast.

Germany advanced toward Russia by land: the margraves of Brandenburg subdued the tribes between the Elbe and the Oder. Western culture and Christianity penetrated into Bohemia, Poland, and Hungary. But the religious organization of Russia was received from the schismatic Greeks It was Constantinople that converted the great Prince Wladimir, at the close of the ninth century. It was now settled that Russia would not, like Poland and Bohemia, enter the system of the Western Church. On the other hand, as she was separated from Constantinople by masses of barbarians, she did not, like the Slavs of the Balkans, place herself under the protection of the Greek Empire. She thus indicated that she was something new and original. This, however, was only the first uncertain gleam. Russia dissolved into principalities and republics. In the thirteenth century she fell almost entirely under the sway of the Mongols. Asia spread over Europe, and wrested Russia from her.

Europe continued to advance. Scandinavians, Germans, and Poles overcame the barrier formed by the tribes of the Baltic. The Swedes took possession of Finland; the Germans, of Livonia and Prussia. The Russians were now in direct contact with the West. At one time the whole coast from the Gulf of Finland to Pomerania belonged to the Teutonic Order, whose grand-master was a vassal of the Pope and of the Emperor. But in the fifteenth century Poland, which was then united to Lithuania, placed herself between Germany and Russia, and wrested from the Muscovite empire a vast extent of territory. It then seemed that Poland was to have the honor of representing the Slavic race in Europe in the form of a great and independent state.

Nevertheless, Russia disengaged herself from the embrace of the Mongols. In the fourteenth century a new state was formed around Moscow, which had regained its independence. While this new state was subordinating to its sway Russian principalities, it encroached upon European Mongolia, fragments of which were to survive long afterward north of the Euxine. Finally, when the Greek Empire disappeared, the Tsar was the heir of the Greek schism and, at the same time, the representative of Eastern Christianity against the infidels, and by this two-fold right he was successor of the Byzantine Cæsar. He saw before him a great future.

§ 17. *Modern Russia.*

During the sixteenth and seventeenth centuries the conflict between the Germans, Scandinavians, and Poles continued without interruption on the shores of the Baltic. The Russians intervened several times with an energy which revealed their desire to occupy this territory, but Sweden was at the summit of her strength. She converted the Baltic into a Swedish lake. Russia, finding the route blocked in this direction, began to recover from Lithuania and Poland a part of the land that she had lost. But it was toward the East and the South that she made the greatest progress. The conquest of the khanates of Kazan and Astrakhan extended her frontier to the Caspian. Though the khans of the Crimea still cut off communication with the Black Sea, the supremacy of the Tsar was extended over the Cossacks of the Don, and the conquest of Siberia was begun.

In the eighteenth century the Russian colossus prospered upon the ruins of Sweden, Poland, and

Turkey. From the first of these countries she took Livonia, Esthonia, Ingria, and portions of Carelia and Finland; from the second, the old Russian Lithuanian provinces and a large part of the Polish territory; from the third, the Crimea and the country between the Bug and the Dniester. At the same time Russia encroached upon Persia, and acquired Georgia first, and then the country of the Khirgiz. Henceforth she had access to the Baltic and the Black Sea. She was near the heart of Europe, and also extended to the heart of Asia. She was the only country of the Continent that could increase indefinitely by absorbing barbarian lands. Her Asiatic empire was contiguous to Europe, and consisted of a connected, natural, and, one might almost say, inevitable aggregation of peoples and territories.

§ 18. *Characteristics of Russia.*

At the close of the period of the Middle Ages we enumerated the states which had been added to Europe. In the modern period two new states appeared: the United Provinces, whose power was of short duration, and Russia, a country with a great future. But did Russia really form a part of Europe?

In the ninth century, when Western Europe, ruled by the learned Carolingians, was deliberating in synods and assemblies on important matters, the Slavs of the Russian plain, in their wretched villages, were barbarians, in fact, almost savages. In the thirteenth century, when France, in the fulness of mediæval civilization, was governed by St. Louis, whose political motto was " Deprive no one of his right," Russia obeyed the Golden Horde, whose capital was a wooden town on the banks of the Volga.

At the close of the fifteenth century, in the period of the Renaissance, Ivan the Terrible caused to be decapitated, or decapitated with his own hand, thousands of his victims, whom he afterward commended to the prayers of the Church. In the seventeenth century were the Russians—those men with long, flowing beards and garments, those women hidden under veils in closed litters—the contemporaries of Louis XIV. ? Peter the Great suppressed their beards and veils, but he did not change their natures ; nor did he desire to do this. He introduced into his empire the instruments of administrative exploitation and the expedients of war employed in Europe ; but he remained the Tsar, the lord with unrestricted power, the father who was addressed as "Thou," like God, and who was obeyed like God. Against his power no other was pitted—no burghers who sounded the belfry bell and stretched chains across street corners ; no body of judges who, while charged with

the administration of the law, defended it against
arbitrary power; no class of nobles whose pride
of blood at times went to their heads, and who
preferred war to the indignity of servile obedience.
In Russia a person was a slave or a noble, but a
person was noble because he served, and in proportion to the extent of his service.   In this immense
country an ignorant clergy chanted prayers which
they did not understand, and lighted candles before images, which the masses adored with heads
bowed to the earth.

Russia had entered the sphere of European
affairs, but she was not a part of Europe.   She
was something different : she was Russia.

§ 19. *Concluding   Reflections—The   Three   Re-gions.*

At the beginning of modern times England was
confined to her island; France and Spain were
commencing to expand abroad; Holland came
into existence, and took her place among the states
that were of importance; Germany and Italy
were in disorder; the Scandinavian states had
been drawn into general history by the contest
for the Baltic and by the Reformation; Poland
was strong; Bohemia and Hungary still maintained their independence; and Turkey was ad-

vancing with vigorous strides. Russia had not
yet found a place among the European powers.

All these states during the modern period were
brought into mutual relation by politics and war.
There was thenceforth one Europe, the individual
members of which knew each other and each
other's designs, entered into alliances when they
had common interests, and fought when their interests conflicted.

Nevertheless, Europe was divided into three
very distinct political regions: England, Western
Europe, and Eastern Europe.

§ 20. *Western Europe.*

The history of Western Europe was dominated
by the consequences of matrimonial politics. During two centuries this region was disturbed because Maximilian, Archduke of Austria, had married the daughter of Charles the Bold, Duke of
Burgundy, and had united his son to Joan the Mad,
heiress of Spain. Spain and France exhausted
themselves in mutual combat, the one to guard
the benefits of family alliances, the other to ward
off the dangers which these alliances involved,
and to remove the obstacles which they placed
in the way of her growth. All these efforts,
wars, and negotiations, in which great princes,
statesmen, and generals distinguished themselves,

ended in little more than the restoration of the *statu quo ante bellum.* Spain and Austria again became distinct powers; Spain was confined to her old limits; France remained what she had been, with some additions of territory; and the Netherlands belonged, as before, to neither of the two rivals. This was certainly a meagre result! It is a mistake to admire so ardently what the epitomes of history call "the grand politics of modern times."

These politics were evolved in a time near our own. They are clearly revealed in the full light of history. We know the actors therein intimately, through the information which they have given concerning themselves, or which others have handed down to us. Almost all of them have a certain charm, and some are great personages. The documents of the period are not merely easy to read; many of them are French classics. It is for this reason that we are apt to exaggerate the importance of the episodes of this period of history.

After the lapse of some hundreds of years, when these glorious wars and great treaties are viewed with a proper perspective, the historian will not assign an important place in the general history of the world to these two centuries, which Western Europe put to such poor use.

In fact, after the Western states had settled their quarrels, it was found that the interest of history lay elsewhere—in the extreme West, where England was becoming the great colonial power; and in the East, where certain powers, old and new, were gaining ground.

§ 21. *Eastern Europe.*

The organization of the East is, on the whole, the capital fact of modern times. In the Middle Ages the East was the scene of irregular efforts and brilliant improvisations. It is true that the kingdoms of Hungary, Bohemia, and Poland had been formed in this region; and that they, together with the Scandinavian states, which were necessarily implicated in the affairs of the East on account of the Baltic, constituted a series of new entities. But the colonization of the coasts had been accomplished in a disorderly way, the work having been divided between the Scandinavians and the Germans; the latter had founded two knightly states, which, though reduced in extent and decaying, still subsisted in the fifteenth century. In the Southeast, Turkey completed the incoherent and picturesque aspect of the East at the close of the Middle Ages.

At the close of the modern period all these states were in decay, or had ceased to exist. Poland had died of political anarchy, which had been cynically nourished by her neighbors. Bohemia and Hungary were dependencies of the Austrian monarchy.

Sweden had been, in the seventeenth century—even earlier than Prussia—a state organized for the production of an army; but the kings over-taxed the country's strength, and expended their energies upon enterprises that were too extensive. Prussia's ambition, on the other hand, was always directed to some precise, circumscribed, and very tangible object; as soon as an advantage was attainable, she attained it. There was always something chimerical and adventurous, after the Norman fashion, in Swedish ambition. Sweden attempted to dominate Germany, to arrest the progress of Russia, to make the Baltic a Swedish lake; her king wished to become King of Poland. This was going too far, and Charles XII. lost his army on the steppes of Russia. Then, as if realizing the prediction made at Vienna at the beginning of the Thirty Years' War, the snow-king melted.

Turkey inundated Europe in the sixteenth century, in the first fervor of her success. Afterward she defended herself and maintained her position, with some fortunate returns to the offensive, thanks to a military organization which was barbarous but very potent. This organization gradually declined. When the janissaries married and became fathers of families, they ceased to be a formidable military force, and Turkey became enervated.

On this foundation of decayed and ruined states

Prussia, Russia, and Austria were aggrandized. These three military powers divided the East among themselves, and substituted, after their fashion, order for chaos. Hence their destinies were, to a certain extent, associated. Together they modified the political history of Europe by breaking down the preponderance of France. This they accomplished by destroying or weakening the kingdoms which French state-craft held at the end of its guiding - strings, namely, Sweden, Poland, and Turkey.

Thus there was an Eastern Europe massed against Western Europe, but divided against itself. The ambitions of the Eastern courts were discordant. After the suppression of the intermediate countries, Prussia and Austria bordered on Russia, while Austria and Russia approached each other along the Danube. To whom shall the spoils of Turkey fall? Who shall have the honor of awakening the people who were asleep under the Ottoman yoke? Of the three partners in the division of Poland, which one will prevail over the other two? The kings of Prussia, successors of the margraves of the North, and the Hapsburg emperors, successors of the margraves of the East, trafficked with the Slavic enemy, and extended the German frontier; but they brought the Russian frontier nearer to theirs. Who made the best bargain, Prussia, Austria, or Russia? The three potentates who had been guilty of this dreadful abuse of power were occupied with the partition of Poland at the moment when the era of the French Revolution dawned upon the world.

§ 22. *New Manners and New Ideas.*

The political history of modern times is thus replete with war. It certainly has some admirable pages. It moves us when it is animated by religious passions, and when there are martyrs in the multitude of the slain. It interests us when it shows either the development of a nation, like France or England, or the creation of an artificial state, like Prussia. It displays the employment of the natural gifts of the different countries, and the operation of genius, discipline, and courage. But it is without principles, without the restraint of probity or honor, without generosity, and without pity. The nations dwelt together like men in the state of nature. The last great political act of Europe before the French Revolution was an assassination, tranquilly premeditated and executed in cold blood.

The intellectual and moral life of modern times was, however, preparing the way for the introduction of other ideas into politics.

Since the fifteenth century manners had been softened and polished. Men and castles had been divested of the habiliments of war; the chevalier had become a cavalier, and the tournament a carousal. The denizens of the castles and communes, who in former times had been isolated from their fellow-men, acquired a taste for "society" and "politeness." Art—formerly the product of guilds—philosophy, literature, and science—formerly the property of the Church and the schools —emerged from these privileged bodies, and were freely diffused throughout society.

The Renaissance studied man and nature, and won them back from the dominion of faith and from the disinclination to observe. In the common effort for the attainment of truth, every country accomplished something; but a common spirit, international by its very name—humanism —circulated everywhere.

The expression of the human mind in the Middle Ages had been scholasticism, that is to say, the interpretation of texts; the expression of the humanistic spirit was reason, that is to say, the affirmation of truth, evident or demonstrated. Reason could not fail to be revolutionary, because it denied tradition and built on a *tabula rasa*. It seemed at first to be entirely disinterested, lofty, and serene, but very soon it stooped to regard life, manners, and politics. Finding these unreasonable, it began to wage war against unreason, and became the philosophy of the eighteenth century.

This new power was dangerous. Though ap-
plying itself to practical life, it remained absolute ;
it was also ignorant, not knowing the historical
legitimacy of existing things. It did not compre-
hend the cathedrals, and it enveloped their origin, or, rather, the causes of their origin, in very
frivolous disdain for " Gothic barbarism." It did
not discern the various nations, and it claimed to
impose upon all humanity, as upon a single real
being, the uniformity of its principles and the banality of common sense. These errors were to be
cruelly expiated. But we should not forget the
beneficial results of " philosophy."

While the thought of the eighteenth century
was active in each of the countries of Europe, it
was also, in various ways, preparing profound mod-
ifications in international relations. The theories
of the economists concerning the efficacy, dignity,
and freedom of labor, their *laissez faire, laissez
passer*, were the absolute contradiction of the
old commercial policy. The idea everywhere expressed and imposed upon the kings, that sovereignty was not property of which a person had
the usufruct, but a magistracy prescribing duties,
was lowering the prince to the second plane, was
placing the country above him, and was, sooner
or later, to substitute for the politics of the sovereigns that of the nations. Philosophy, by preach-
ing tolerance and rejecting religion, was seculariz-

ing politics. Finally, philosophy was preparing, |
in a confused way, a future of innovations, by its
general and generous ideas of humanity and justice; by utopias, like that of the Abbé de Saint-
Pierre ; by the very prejudices against the past; by
thoughtless hatred of all customs and the alliance
of sarcasm against " the traces of barbarism ; " by
the affirmation that " things cannot continue as
they are," and that the next generations " will see
great things; " by the *Adveniat regnum tuum*
addressed to " the light."

At the close of the eighteenth century France
no longer guided general European politics. The
last two great conflicts—the War of the Austrian
Succession and the Seven Years' War—had been
disastrous to her; the second of these had impaired her fame. By land and by sea the power
of France was curtailed. The revenge that she
wreaked on England, in the American War of Independence, did not compensate for her earlier disasters. That war was, however, something else
than an act of reprisal. It was the work of the
new spirit, a very noble action undertaken with
sincere enthusiasm. France had declined in the
old political world ; but it was she who had de-
nounced and disowned that world with the greatest energy. She held, and was about to sound, the
trumpet of judgment.

CHAPTER V.

§ 1. *Destruction of Europe.*

No country ever influenced Europe as France did between 1789 and 1815. Impelled by two dreams—the dream of a war against the kings on behalf of the people, and the dream of the foundation of an empire of the Cæsarian or Carolingian type—the French armies overran the Continent, and trampled under foot, as they went, much rank vegetation, which has never risen again.

Non-commissioned officers promoted to the rank of generals, dukes, and kings, and a subaltern who became emperor, were novelties compared with generals taken from the ranks of lords, archdukes, and princes. The former emerged, fully armed, not from a court, but from the very marrow of a people. Both generals and emperor attacked ancient institutions. The generals threw into the Rhine the mitres of the electoral archbishops, and covered Italy, the classic land of tyrants, with republics. The emperor, on the day of the battle of

Austerlitz, destroyed the Holy Roman Empire of
the German Nation.   Some years later he decreed
that "whereas" the temporal power bestowed by
Charlemagne, his "glorious predecessor," upon
the Pope was being put to a bad use, it should
be taken from him.

Napoleon covered the Revolution with an ar-
chæological mantle. The recollections of Rome
haunted his memory only less than those of Charlemagne, whose name he often uttered. The last
gleams of the past penetrated to him, mingling
with his glory and deranging his mind; but the
Revolution imbued him.. He served it when he
disembroiled the chaos of Germany, when he made
Northern Italy a kingdom, when he imprisoned
the Pope who had been forced to crown him in
Notre-Dame, and when he vaguely thought of
wresting Poland from the eagles that were sharing
her territory. He also served it, despite and in
opposition to himself, when, oppressing Europe to
satisfy his caprice, he aroused the souls of the
Spaniards and the Germans. He was the Revolution and the destroyer of the ancient régime, to
such an extent that his fall was followed by a
return to the offensive on the part of old Europe.
The great despot was saluted during his captivity
in St. Helena as a deliverer, and was venerated as
such after his death, because he had made pope,
emperor, and tsar tremble.

§ 2. *Restoration of Europe.*

After their victory, in 1815, the old monarchies repaired, as well as they could, the Europe that France had shattered. The East was restored almost to the condition in which it had been in the eighteenth century. The grand - duchy of Warsaw, which was an attempt to reconstruct Poland, vanished. Russia and Austria remained the vanguards of Europe against Turkey, which continued to lose ground. Italy was again divided among princes, dominated over by Austria, which seemed to recover the old imperial rights over the Peninsula. Spain regained her wretched dynasty. England, which had been the leading spirit in the formation of a permanent coalition against France, was more than ever the undisputed sovereign of the seas. Thus the work of the Revolution appeared to be destroyed.

Nevertheless, the restoration was not complete. Austria did not recover Belgium; the latter was united to Holland, in order that the kingdom of the Netherlands should have considerable weight along the frontier of France. Germany could not be restored to her three hundred princes, for most of those that the Revolution and the Empire had crushed, remained buried in the ruins. Germany, which before the Revolution was neither a

monarchial nor a feudal nor a federal state, became a confederation with thirty-nine members.
This confederation contained within itself the
germs of death; for the princes were the only
ones who had any weight in its councils, and
they were very unequal in power. Prussia, aggrandized, and charged with the defence of the
Rhine against France, was more than ever the
rival of Austria, whose old titles to glory and pre-
eminence had given her the presidency of the Diet
at Frankfort. But badly constituted as she was,
Germany had been simplified. She felt that she
was nearer the great object of the ambition of
her patriots, who aspired to become a nation.

Thus the old régime was not able to recover
possession of the whole of Europe. The treaties
of 1815 accepted accomplished facts. Whatever
their work was, the princes found it good, *vi-
derunt quod esset bonum.* Like the Creator, they
wished to rest, after having appointed the Holy
Alliance guardian of reconstructed Europe. But
ideas had been diffused through the world that
were to engender new revolutions.

§ 3. *Patriotism of the Revolution.*

Excepting England, a country of slow and con-
tinuous transformations, in which the present is not
separated from the past by visible lines of demar-

cation, Europe has been transformed since the Revolution. Before 1789 she had no real nations. At the present day they are abundant.

In France, the loyalty of the nobility, a very noble sentiment, and the love of the people for the king, a very touching sentiment, used to take the place of patriotism. When, owing to the faults of its kings, the country detached itself from royalty, it raised itself all at once to the idea of humanity. French writers of the eighteenth century rediscovered this idea, which had been lost since the time of Plato, Seneca, and Marcus Aurelius, or, at least, had been replaced in the Middle Ages by the ecclesiastical idea of Christianity, and later on by the political idea of Europe.

The Revolution created the fatherland, or *patria*, as we understand the term at the present day. In vain had the revolutionists been the disciples of the philosophers, in vain had they guided themselves by general principles and made laws of pure reason; in spite of their philosophy, they were French patriots. For the kingdom of France they substituted the French nation—in other words, a moral entity for a political expression. They declared the national soil to be sacred and indivisible, treated emigration as a crime, invasion as a sacrilege, and proclaimed, with tragic enthusiasm and tocsin-like declamation, that all men owed a duty to their native country in time of danger.

§ 4. *The Principle of Nationality.*

Nevertheless, on becoming self-conscious, the French nation could not escape the effects of its philosophical education. In the code of principles forming the " Declaration of the Rights of Man," France did not legislate merely for her own benefit. The " Declaration" asserts that "the principle of all sovereignty resides in the nation." Whence it follows that the nations, being collective entities composed of men who desire to live under the same laws, ought neither to be governed by foreigners nor to be incorporated, wholly or in part, with foreign states : they are independent and indivisible. Moreover, they are free. " Law is the expression of the general will. All citizens have the right to co-operate personally or by their representatives in its formation." The nation, as thus defined, forms an absolute contrast with the states of former times, which grouped together, but did not unite, nations or fragments of various nations, no one of which made its own laws.

These two maxims of the " Declaration " have, in part, guided the history of our century.

In the sixteenth, and even in the seventeenth, century there were international religious parties ; in the nineteenth century political parties and passions overstep the frontiers. The Holy Alliance of sovereigns was " international." Its purpose was to maintain the work of reaction accomplished at Vienna against the principle of nationality based upon consent and that of political freedom. In every country of Europe this Alliance had adherents and also opponents, the latter known as " nationalists" or " liberals." The conflict between the two camps was directed by France.

Since the Revolution France has lived in a state of political instability. Her enemies and even her own sons have reproached her for the number of her constitutions and for her periodical revolutions. Nevertheless, if she needs more than a century to establish herself firmly under the new régime, it should not cause much astonishment. The English Revolution, properly understood, lasted longer. But, amid all these fluctuations, France has had fixed ideas. Though faithless once to the cause of political freedom, the ways of which are not to be learned in fifty years, she is constantly progressing as a democracy. On the other hand, she has defended against all comers, even against her own interests, the principle of nationality. That is why she has been, during the greater part of this century, a motive power. Her liberals have set the fashion for the liberals of Europe ; her revolutions have disturbed the whole Continent. Those of 1830 and 1848 emboldened liberals and nationalists of all countries ; nor did the year 1851 discourage the latter.   Since 1870 France has represented, more than ever, the principles of freedom and nationality.

§ 5. *The New Nations.*

Let us now consider what obstacles were ob-structing the principle of nationality in 1815. Belgium had been united, against her will, to Hol-land.   The assignment of Holstein to the King of Denmark had placed Germans under the govern-ment of a Dane.   Germany and Italy had been divided into sovereign states that were hostile to every form of national constitution; moreover, one of the fairest portions of the territory of Italy was under the Austrian yoke.   Poland was divided among three states; Bohemia and Hungary re-mained incorporated, without special rights, in the Austrian empire; on the Danube and in the Balkan Peninsula various nationalities were under the government of the Sultan.   Thus the most formidable powers were leagued against the new principle.

Nevertheless, it has made great progress. Europe of 1891 no longer resembles that of 1815. Greece was the first to recover her national life, and Belgium has been separated from Holland. The German duchies have been taken from the King of Denmark.   Hungary has secured a constitution of her own in the Austrian monarchy. Germany and Italy, those victims of the priesthood and the Empire, have become nations; and, by an inevitable vicissitude of fortune, Italy has shut up the Pope in the Vatican, and Germany has cast from her bosom the successor of the emperors. Some concessions have also been made to the national sentiment of the Slavic countries of the Austrian realm. Finally, out of dismembered Turkey have emerged, as separate nations, Roumania, Servia, and Montenegro; while Bulgaria and Roumelia now recognize the suzerainty of the Sultan only by the payment of a tribute, and are at present serving the apprenticeship of their independence.

There are some admirable pages in the history of these revolutions. The Hellenic outbreak was aided by poetic sentiments—admiration for the heroes of this war of independence, and gratitude to a country that has been such an honor to humanity. The Belgian revolution was a double application of the principle of nationality. The Belgians began by separating themselves from a state under whose laws they did not wish to live; then, in spite of affinities of race and language that drew them toward France, they secured for themselves a separate national life.

The Slavic nationalities regained a consciousness of their existence before claiming the right to exist.

The songs of their ancient poets, the narrations of their historians, and the legends of their remote past revealed them to themselves, so that their patriotic writers, whether philologists or historians, may be considered founders of states. This is something new in the world.

Herein, then, we find the great characteristic of our century. A principle — not, as formerly, a prince's convenience, a marriage, a bequest, or the ambition to gain victories and to conquer—has caused several wars, the result of which has been, not territorial acquisition and the destruction of peoples, but the reconstruction of old, and the creation of new, nations.

The principle of nationality has thus achieved victories, but the most violent combats remain to be fought. There are various reasons for believing that its complete and final triumph will be prevented.

§ 6. *Definition of " Nationality "—Imperfection of National Development.*

In the first place, the subject is obscured by uncertainty as to the definition of the term "nationality." Among the French a nationality is regarded as the work of history, ratified by the will of man. The elements composing it may be very different in their origin. The point of departure is of little importance ; the only essential thing is the point reached.

The Swiss nationality is the most complete. It embraces three families of people, each of which speaks its own language. Moreover, since the Swiss territory belongs to three geographical regions, separated by high mountains, Switzerland, which has vanquished the fatality of nature, from both the ethnographical and geographical point of view, is a unique and wonderful phenomenon. But she is a confederation, and for a long time has been a neutral country. Thus her constitution has not been subjected to the great ordeal of fire and sword.

France, despite her diverse races—Celtic, German, Roman, and Basque—has formed a political entity that most resembles a moral person. The Bretons and the Alsacians, who do not all understand the language of her government, have not been the least devoted of her children in the hour of tribulation. Among the great nations France is the nation *par excellence.* Elsewhere the nationality blends, or tends to blend, with the race, a natural development and, hence, one devoid of merit.

All the countries that have not been able to unite their races into a nation, have a more or less troubled existence. Prussia has not been able to nationalize (that is the proper word to use) her

Polish subjects; hence she has a Polish question, not to mention at present any other. England has an Irish question. Both Turkey and Austria have a number of such questions. Groups of people in various parts of the Austrian Empire demand from the Emperor that they may be allowed to live as Germans, Hungarians, Tsechs, Croatians, in fact, even as Italians. They do not revolt against him; on the contrary, each of them offers him a crown. The time is, however, past when a single head can wear several crowns; to-day every crown is heavy.

These race claims are not merely a cause of internal troubles; the agitations that they arouse may lead to great wars. Evidently no state will ever interpose between Ireland and England; but, while quarrels take place between Germans and Slavs, there will intervene the two conflicting forces of Pan-Germanism and Pan-Slavism, formidable results and final consequences of ethnographical patriotism.

Pan-Germanism and Pan-Slavism are, indeed, not forces officially acknowledged and organized. The Emperor of Germany can honestly deny that he is a Pan-Germanist, and the Tsar that he is a Pan-Slavist. Germans and Slavs of Austria, and Slavs of the Balkans, may, for their part, desire to remain Austrian or independent, as they are to-day. It is none the less true, however, that there is in Europe an old quarrel between two great

races, that each of them is represented by a powerful empire, and that these empires cannot forever
remain unconcerned about the quarrels of the two
races.

§ 7. *Application of the Principle of Nationality to Italy.*

The chief application of the principle of nationality has been the formation of the Italian
and German nations.   In former times the existence, in the centre of the Continent, of two objects
of greed was a permanent cause of war.   Will the
substitution of two important states for German
anarchy and Italian polyarchy prove a guaranty
of future peace ?

We must distinguish between · Germany and
Italy.   The national revolution has been accomplished in a very different way in the two countries.

Italian unity is almost completed, for the number of Italians remaining outside the new kingdom
is not great.   On the other hand, this nation con-
tains only Italians.   The union was accomplished
for the profit of a prince, the King of Piedmont,
who certainly had claims to the honor.   Moreover,
he was not powerful enough to make the unification resemble a conquest of the Peninsula by the
Piedmontese.   In fact, after the inhabitants of the

various principalities had given their assent to the union, Piedmont disappeared in the nation, and Victor Emmanuel ceased to be King of Piedmont on becoming King of Italy. Finally, the Italian nationality came into existence without any violation of the principle of nationality. France, in compensation for her sacrifices, obtained Savoy and the county of Nice. But the sovereign of these countries, who granted them to the French, had not been conquered by the French; he had been conqueror in company with them and with their help. Moreover, the inhabitants of Savoy and the county of Nice formally consented to become Frenchmen. Thus the new law was here applied in all its tenor. But let us consider the results.

On becoming a great power, Italy desired to have the army, the navy, and the policy of a great power. Wisdom, perhaps, directed this new nation to taste tranquilly the joy of feeling herself grow, after having experienced the joy of feeling herself come into being. But she did not have complete possession of herself. She was not entirely in her own home like the other nations. All the soil between the Alps and the promontories of Sicily is not Italian. In the centre of this region stands a palace surrounded with a garden: it is the domain of St. Peter. Here the King of Italy does not enter.

The Apostle Peter is a victim of the principle of nationality, which he does not recognize, for he regards the nations merely as provinces of the Church.   Hence he claims his property, which he received from King Pipin, and which Charlemagne confirmed to him by placing on his tomb "the charter of donation."   Since that time eleven centuries have passed, but eleven centuries do not count in the immutability of the Church.   In the course of the ages the domain of Peter has often been assailed, never, however, without the assailant having cause to repent.   Bourbon, the Constable of France, was killed before Rome's walls.   No one fell in 1870 at the assault of Porta Pia, but punishment is not always immediately inflicted on "crime."   The King of the Lombards, in the eighth century, and Napoleon I., in the nineteenth, waited some years before it was meted out to them.

The Pope, though shut up in the Vatican, has continued his broad survey of the world; in fact, since the Middle Ages, his horizon has widened. Everywhere on the globe there are Catholics; and in several countries of Europe they form a party, which the governments, however strong they may be, are obliged to take into account.   The Emperor of Germany is very potent, but when he visited the King of Italy, it was beyond his power to refuse to pay his respects to the Pope.   The Emperor of Austria calls himself the good brother and special friend of Humbert I., but he does not visit Rome for fear of committing sacrilege.

Nevertheless, the Apostle does not cease to upbraid and lament. The plaintive cry of the immortal old prelate sounds like an unceasing knell above Rome, the Italian capital. It disturbs and irritates king and ministers. What is the use of being in Rome only to find one's self still face to face with a Roman question? From time to time people fear, or pretend to fear, that the Franks may once more descend from the mountains to drive away the Lombards.

Accordingly Italy sought, where she expected to find it, an assurance against all intervention in favor of the Holy See. This precaution she had the right to take. But every alliance costs something, and those that Italy has contracted have cost much. Then, after having been guided by solicitude for her safety, it appears that she was misled by dreams. It is very difficult to refrain from dreaming a little on the top of the Capitol. The conquerors who mounted there in triumph called the Mediterranean *mare nostrum*. Among the spoils that they presented to Jupiter were, on one occasion, those of Carthage.

Thus to the Roman question Italy has added that of the Mediterranean. Down to the present time questions of this sort have not been settled peacefully.

§ 8. *Application of the Principle of Nationality to Germany.*

The unification of Germany differs entirely from that of Italy. It is not completed, for several million Germans were excluded from their fatherland by the Treaty of Prague, which left Austria out of the new state. The new Germany does not contain Germans only: in 1866 Prussia added to it her part of Poland and a Danish country, and, in 1870, certain French provinces. This unification, which allowed the parody of a confederation to subsist, was accomplished by the German prince who had most claims to the honor. But the King of Prussia had acquired, during the last century and a half, the rank and power of a European prince. He was the successor of statesmen and conquerors each of whom had added to the domain of their house a certain number of square miles. Thus the unification of Germany assumed the character of a conquest by Prussia. In fact, it was in virtue of the right of conquest, officially appealed to, that Schleswig - Holstein, Hanover, Frankfort, and Hesse-Cassel were united to Prussia. The constitution of 1866 was drawn up by a conqueror for the conquered. It was completed in 1870; but the King of Prussia, who was proclaimed Emperor at Versailles, remained King of

Prussia. Prussia, thus aggrandized, presses with all her weight on Germany, imposing upon the whole Empire her peculiar spirit, the spirit of a military state.

Finally, victorious Germany inflicted a wound upon France that will never be forgotten.

§ 9. *The Alsacian Question.*

At the conclusion of a history of thirty centuries, in which the attempt has been made to discriminate the most important facts, one must not be tempted to exaggerate or to misinterpret an event merely because it has wounded one's feelings. Indeed, the injuries that have been inflicted upon Germany by French politics in the past are well known. A French historian must recognize that Germany had an absolute right to adopt such measures as were best adapted to protect her against the French. But her unification and vengeance were accomplished together in such a way that the peace of the world will long be menaced.

It is difficult to make foreigners understand why France cannot resign herself to the loss of her provinces. "It is the law of war," say the Germans. Such language would not have surprised anyone in the last century; and even to - day it seems natural to statesmen of the old régime.

But, in the present century, France represents another policy.

Among all the nations of the world she is pre-eminently rationalistic and sensitive. She thinks that it is not proper to treat an aggregate of men like a herd of cattle. She believes in the existence of a people's soul. She has manifested sorrow and sympathy for the sufferings of the victims of force. She has wept over Athens, Warsaw, and Venice, and has not given the "oppressed" merely tears. If France assisted the United Provinces to secure freedom in the seventeenth century, it was only a fortunate result of the policy of her kings; but when the French shed their blood to deliver the United States, Greece, Belgium, and Italy, it was an intentional result of new sentiments.

The Peace of Frankfort did not bequeath to the French merely the humiliation of defeat. It did not merely open their frontier, and place their country in a condition of intolerable insecurity. In taking from them people that were French, and desired to remain so, the conqueror wounded the French in their convictions. He did not even appeal to ethnographical patriotism. He could not claim Alsace as German; for he took possession of Metz, and retained Schleswig and the Polish countries. He simply used the old right of force. That is what determines the character of the Alsa-

cian question. This question, in fact, places face
to face two stages of civilization; and the French
in their defeat may claim, as a singular honor, that
the redress of the wrong done to them would be a
satisfaction to reason and to the most generous sentiments of our time.

§ 10. *Austrian and Russian Wars of Conquest.*

Thus the introduction of the principle of nationality has not resulted in the destruction of old
political habits.   Even in the nineteenth century
there have been wars of conquest and attempts at
territorial aggrandizement.

Austria and Russia, like Prussia, are conquerors.
Austria is descending the Danube, and is moving
toward Adrianople. It is the direction that was
pointed out to her, more than a thousand years
ago, by the founder of the " Eastern March."
The Hapsburgs forgot this early mission as soon
as their matrimonial politics entangled them in
all the affairs of Western Europe. Italy and
Germany have reminded Austria of it, the one
by forcing her beyond the Alps, the other by de-
priving her of the quality of a German state.
Austria is to-day pre-eminently a Danubian state.
She has taken possession of Bosnia and Herzego-
vina. She is striving to extend her political authority or "influence" over the petty Balkan

states. But this plan is opposed by a powerful adversary.

Russia, in the present century, has made progress at the expense of the Turkish Empire. She employs force and sentiment simultaneously against this state. It was from Constantinople that she originally received Christianity; hence it is incumbent upon her to take from Islam the dome of St. Sophia. She is also the big Slavic brother, who must help her smaller brothers, the subjects of the Sultan. Thus religion and ethnographical patriotism mingle with politics, and give Russia a power of action at present unequalled in the world. But this power is restrained by rivals : the route from St. Petersburg toward the South is crossed by the route from Vienna toward the East. Finally, the question of the Dardanelles is of European and even universal interest. It concerns the balance of power between the two greatest dominions in the world, that of England and that of Russia.

§ 11. *Expansion of Europe.*

In recent times Europe has continued to extend her sway over the world. At the present day she is completing this process. There is nothing more for her to seize in America; but she has thrown herself upon the Dark Continent and Asia.

In Africa, the new powers, Germany and Italy, seek that position outside of Europe which seems to be the natural complement of every power of any importance. A state is not considered great if the statesmen and newspapers cannot speak of "our colonial empire." In Africa, the old powers, England and France, are expanding most rapidly, the latter toward the north and west, the former toward the south and east. In Asia, France has appropriated her share. At present, however, Asia is mainly Chinese, English, and Russian. There the Russian glacier is always gliding onward.

Since 1815 the distant seas and continents have not heard the cannonade of Europeans against Europeans. At present the occupation of the world is, as it seems, being peacefully completed. Diplomatic commissions proceed amicably with their demarcations. They trace grand lines on the docile paper. In fact, an innovation in the form of an international state has been established. By common consent, Christians have entered into an alliance against the slave-dealer, just as they formerly did against the infidel. All proceeds peacefully, all for civilization. Some years ago, however, the world almost witnessed a duel between "the whale and the white bear," because the progress of Russia toward the Indian frontier disturbed England. The occupation of some unimportant islets almost caused a conflict between

Germany and Spain. There is friction, even at the present day, between England and Portugal on account of a bay in East Africa. What will happen when all the attainable territory is occupied and the states are neighbors in the different parts of the world, it is not difficult to conjecture, when one considers what for centuries have been their relations as neighbors on the Continent.

Here, as everywhere, there are indications of war. Has our century then failed to keep the promises which it seems to have made? Just what has been its work compared with that of preceding centuries? What tasks does it bequeath to the future? We shall attempt, by way of conclusion, to answer these questions.

§ 12. *Past and Present Politics.*

Several traits of earlier politics have been effaced or weakened in the present century.

Royal families still enter into marriage alliances, but the political effects are unimportant. Denmark and Germany excel in disposing of their princesses; but it was of no service to Denmark, in 1864, that the crown-princes of England and Russia were the sons-in-law of the Danish King. Greece will not become the vassal of the German

Empire because her heir-apparent has married the sister of William II.

Several countries have summoned foreigners to rule over them; but these princes, begotten by fertile Germany, must be Belgian in Brussels, Roumanian in Bucharest, and Bulgarian in Sophia.

Thus the importance of royal families and kings has diminished, and the nations have come to the foreground.

Religious affinities and aversions still determine certain currents in politics. There exists an international papal question. The Eastern Question is complicated by strong religious passions. Nevertheless, religion has lost the international position that it occupied in the sixteenth and seventeenth centuries.

The ambition of territorial aggrandizement is tempered by a certain modesty. At the present day no sovereign would dare to undertake annexations on pretexts such as Louis XIV. gave before attacking Spain, in 1667, or Frederick II., in 1740, after invading Silesia. If Poland's existence, miserable as it was, had been prolonged a few decades, her destruction would, perhaps, have been impossible.

War is no longer, as in the preceding period, the normal condition of Europe; years of peace are no longer the exception. Very serious motives

11

are now necessary for a declaration of war. The combats of our century have been worth the trouble of fighting. But this is not a reason for believing that the time is approaching when every nation will be able to repose under its own vine and fig-tree, unarmed and free from care.

§ 13. *Causes of Peace.*

Let us place in one of the scales of a balance the causes of peace.

First, there is the spirit of the French Revolution. By destroying the property right of the sovereign over the people and over the country, by creating the theory of the nation based upon national consent, and by proclaiming the dignity of human beings, the Revolution has rendered difficult certain kinds of war.

Then, there is the universal progress of labor; the heat of the forge, and the feverish enterprise of the counting-room; the circulation of persons, ideas, and interests between different countries; a general solidarity in the effort to acquire wealth; and unanimity in the desire to enjoy one's possessions in peace.

Finally, there is a feeling opposed to war, with which are blended a certain new ideal of engineers and inventors, fear of the inconveniences and dan-

gers of military life, survivals of old and noble
Christian or philosophic ideas, and sentiments of
humanity.

§ 14. . *Causes of War.*

Let us now place in the other scale the causes
of war.

Here, too, we find the spirit of the Revolution.
The principle of nationality will not be satisfied
until it conquers England, Germany, and Russia,
and destroys Austria and Turkey. It will not
accomplish all these objects, but it will seek to attain some of them. Supposing that it destroys
Austria and Turkey, what battle-fields will arise
on their ruins !

Among the causes of war we find also the universal progress of labor, and competition in the
pursuit of wealth. It is not true that the development of material interests promotes peace. Commerce, as the messenger of peace, is a mythologi-
cal character. In its origin it was brigandage;
in ancient, mediæval, and modern times it oc-
casioned wars. Men fought on the Baltic for
herring, and on all the seas for spices. In our day
the growth of industries creates the question of
foreign markets, which, in turn, brings the interests of the states into conflict. Commercial rivalry
and rancor thus strengthen national hatred.

Pacific ideas and sentiments are uncertain and frail.   Engineers and inventors do not refuse their services in behalf of war; in fact, they give it a new, scientific, and monstrous character.   True there exist disdain and horror of the military system and the barracks; but war has retained its devotees, and general opinion still tends to place in the first rank the duty which exposes a person to the danger of death.

Finally, the old features of union between countries are being daily effaced.

§ 15. *National Individualism.*

The immense development of commercial intercourse, the hundred-fold increase of ways and means of communication, the medley of financial interests in the exchanges of Paris, London, and Berlin, constitute one of the phenomena of our time; but national individualism is another, of an entirely opposite nature.   Nations have become more estranged from one another, in proportion to the growth of international interests.

The Christian spirit formerly attempted to discipline men by the sentiment of their brotherhood in God; but of this spirit the politics of to-day do not feel the least breath.   The philosophy of the last century brought into fashion the sentiment of

brotherhood in humanity; to-day the most wide-
spread of the systems of philosophy, that which
has permeated the sciences, teaches the necessity
of the conflict for existence and the legitimacy of
the selection made by the work of death.

Formerly certain literatures were dominant in
Europe. That of France was almost universal,
and is still at present, perhaps, the most wide-
spread. It furnishes the theatres of European
capitals with dramas and comedies. But French
dramatic art, though it has power, subtlety, and
grace, is less impersonal than formerly : it is more
varied, more French, more Parisian. There is also
a great circulation of novels throughout the world;
but the novel renounces general themes, preferring
to observe the immediate and the real. We de-
light in finding in foreign writers manners different from our own. Such differences are what always and everywhere appear in their works.

Formerly the ancient classics were, in all countries, the principal means of education. The
humanities were, of course, international ; in fact,
all men of any importance in politics and society
had been the pupils of the same masters. At the
present day we deny to the humanities not merely
the exclusive, but any, right in education. Here
also the modern spirit undertakes the destruction
of the general and universal, and hence is separ-
atistic.

The long evolution begun with the ruin of the Roman Empire, hindered and sometimes arrested by sentiments, ideas, and customs, is in our day being completed; national individualism is now an accomplished fact.

In the last few centuries there was spread over the surface of Europe a veneer of common forms of government and court life, which gave an appearance of similarity. Revolutions have cracked this veneer, and the substitution of nationalities for governments has dissipated the illusion of resemblance. Europe now appears as she really is, with her irreconcilable contrasts, national, ethnological, and chronological. We see this to-day very clearly. From Paris, where the government of the French Republic sits, to Berlin, where the hereditary general-in-chief of the Prussian army rules, and from Berlin to the Kremlin, where the father of Holy Russia is crowned, the distance is measured, not merely by kilometers, a negligible quantity, but also by centuries.

Where individualism is of ethnographical substance it displays its irreconcilable spirit in a naïve way. Hungary is thrown into a violent passion because a flag is placed where it has no right to be. Nowhere is the Tsech willing to hear the German language, neither in the school, nor in the church, nor in the court of law. To be absorbed in one's self, to contemplate and love one's

self, and, when one is proud of one's birth, to admire one's self — that is the psychological condition of a modern people.

§ 16. *Conclusion.*

Thus even the innovations of this century, the
spirit of the Revolution, and the progress of human labor weigh in both scales of the balance.
Moreover, from the past there has been transmitted
the old cause of war, the policy of aggrandizement
and conquest. This policy is very clear and deter-
minate; it is carried on in places that are well defined and visible. The Balkans and the spire of
Strasburg dominate the politics of Europe at the
present day.

This is the reason why the expectation of war is
one of the principal phenomena of our present civilization. It manifests itself in the system of armed
peace. Formerly peace wore only demi-armor; to-
day it is armed from head to foot. Without any
effort, by a tap of the telegraph, after some puffs
of locomotives, there is war; and what a terrible
war! Just as the politics of former centuries appear to be almost trivial compared with those of to-
day, so the armies of Turenne and Condé, compared
with ours, seem to be mere playthings. It was
observed a moment ago that wars are becoming

rarer; but they employ their time to better advantage. Formerly years of fighting were necessary for the capture of a few cities. France
needed only six weeks, and Prussia three, to
precipitate the Italian and German revolutions.
The French pride themselves on having held out
six months against Germany to save their honor.
The feeling, that a few dawns may suffice to il-
lumine the desperate conflict and the death of a
fatherland, weighs heavily upon Europe. There
are countries in which the cruel cry *væ victis* is
ready to burst forth from men's breasts.

In truth, it is not wholly impossible that the ap-
prehension of war retards war. No one is sure of
winning, and everyone knows that defeat may
be fatal. This is what makes the hand hesitate
that is able to give the tap on the telegraph. It is
possible that armed peace, by being prolonged,
may appear at once too burdensome and too ab-
surd, and that reason and humanity may assert
their right. Perhaps, too, it will be necessary to
heed the complaints of "the disinherited" and to
reduce the budgets of war, in order to give the
miners of Flanders, Westphalia, and Silesia a little more time at table and two additional hours of
sleep. But these are very vague hopes.

Moreover, it is a question whether universal
peace is a desirable object, whether it would not
diminish the original energy of national genius,

whether the best way to serve humanity would be to create human banality, whether new virtues would arise to replace the virtues of war. It is also a question whether universal and perpetual peace is not radically and *naturally* impossible. These are profound problems, solvable only by him who may know the beginning and end of things, and hence insolvable. Let us then leave this painful metaphysical aspect of the subject and resolutely consider the possibilities of the future.

At the close of the last century we distinguished three regions of Europe—the Centre and West, England, and Russia—to show that perpetual wars between the states of the first region had made the fortune of the other two. England, in recent times, has considerably extended her colonial territory; she is adding to it daily, and at the present moment she talks of organizing it into an empire. Russia, at the same time that she increases her territory, is gaining strength. Every year she makes more progress. Her wheat-fields and vines multiply the supply of grain and grapes; the fertility of her inhabitants equals that of the soil; new industries are being introduced, and prosper; the credit of the state is being strengthened. All this is done methodically and noiselessly, with the tranquillity that characterizes work performed by the calm forces of nature. Moreover, there is no discord on the Continent that does not serve England and Russia. The Franco-German conflict and the misunderstandings between France and Italy assure to England the security of her domination. The Alsacian question is worth to Russia the doubling of her army. Thus the central powers contribute to the development of the two wings of Europe. The constant progress of her neighbors in the East ought, at least, to make Germany reflect. If she still has political philosophers, they have an excellent subject for study in "the future of Russia." The phenomenon of a great nation, in which wealth and modern forces are increasing, while its spirit remains that of the West at the time of the Crusades, merits their meditation.

Let us now consider the position of Europe in the universe. A century ago she was the only historical entity; to-day there is a second. The most important results of the discoveries of the fifteenth century are now beginning to appear. America is no longer a dependency of the old world. A series of revolutions has transformed the colonies into independent states. Like Europe, America is filled with nations. We say "Europe" to designate a sort of political community; the Americans say "America" with the same intention. America is conscious of the contrast that she forms with political and military Europe, and she is proud of it. This very contrast gives her a sort of unity. It permits bold spirits to speak of *Pan-Americanism.*

The relations between the Old World and the New are not necessarily peaceful. Down to the present, the latter has had no foreign policy; still the Monroe Doctrine, " America for the Americans," is a policy. If it is ever applied to the islands of America (premonitory signs of this are not wanting), it will cause a conflict between the two worlds.

American civilization is pacific. All these new nations grow and multiply in the midst of peace. Peace is thus their vocation, but, as if it were contrary to the eternal order of things, the United States are beginning to use their treasury surplus for the construction of war vessels. Armaments are ruining Europe, while American wealth is producing armaments.

It is not necessary, in concluding, to seek the facile originality of a paradox. After having descended the course of time, one naturally desires to presage the future. After having started so far back in the past, it is impossible to stop short on the threshold of the future. After having seen so many changes, states come into existence and perish, empires crumble that had hoped for eternal life, we must foresee new revolutions, deaths, and births.

All force exhausts itself; the faculty of guiding the course of history is not an inalienable possession. Europe, which inherited it from Asia three thousand years ago, will not, perhaps, retain it forever.

INDEX.